DD571176

"Robin Hemley has traveled to more countries than just about anyone I know, and along the way he's collected vital observations on the tragic absurdity of nationalism and the implicit violence of a world crisscrossed with borders. I think of him in the company of Pankaj Mishra, Pico Iyer, Bruce Chatwin, and John Berger—writers whose transnational souls challenge the idea of a single place of origin."

—JESS ROW, author of *White Flights* and *Your Face in Mine*

"This is a book of daring travel and quiet observation. *Borderline Citizen* challenges common constructs of national borders, patriotism, and citizenship to shed an urgent light on the exile's predicament. With a sharp wit guided by empathy, Hemley has written a necessary and entirely unique book about what it really means to belong in a divided world."

—JENNIFER PERCY, journalist and author of *Demon Camp*

"Robin Hemley is a born traveler, and in *Borderline Citizen* he visits exclaves, enclaves, and places in between to explore what loyalty to and love of a country mean. In Havana and Hong Kong, Kaliningrad and the Falkland Islands, he poses questions about identity, a complicated subject for many in the twenty-first century, and what he learns along the way is by turns illuminating and amazing. Thus a journey to an artificial rain forest in Nebraska inspires a meditation on authenticity, which reveals that in these uncertain times there is no better guide to the challenges we face than Robin Hemley."

—CHRISTOPHER MERRILL, author of *Self-Portrait with Dogwood*

"Few writers have traveled as voraciously as Robin Hemley, and none with his special blend of curiosity, heart, and wit. His latest collection interrogates the idea of nationhood by spotlighting a wide spectrum of citizens—from an Afghan refugee to a Chinese billionaire—to prove that personhood is all that matters in the end. At a time when nationalism is resurging around the globe, Hemley bolsters the spirit with this vibrant read."

—STEPHANIE ELIZONDO GRIEST, author of *All the Agents and Saints: Dispatches from the U.S. Borderlands*

"Someone draws a line and you must not cross it. . . . In Robin Hemley's newest creation, *Borderline Citizen*, he traverses the globe interrogating ideas of home and (inter)national identity. Hemley brings to light the power of place, the echoes of hope even in desolation, and reminds us that in whatever land, there are people living and surviving and loving. This is not a 'grass is always greener' book but rather one that paints the world as always green and should always be green, no matter what shadows that try to dim it."

—IRA SUKRUNGRUANG, author of *Buddha's Dog and Other Meditations*

"With disarming charm and ease, Robin Hemley writes of enclaves and exclaves, incidents and accidents, and serendipitous personal encounters, teasing out important and current questions about the things that divide and bring us together. *Borderline Citizen* is a first-class ticket to understanding the complexities of identity and nation."

—ANGELO R. LACUESTA, author of *City Stories*

"Robin Hemley explodes the very idea of nationhood and in so doing redefines it, offering a more thoughtful and humane notion of how to be a citizen of our world today. These 'dispatches' are travel writing at its best, where the writer delves into the intimacies of foreign places, seeing beyond their exotic surfaces, in search of a global humanity. Brilliantly comic, darkly but poignantly introspective, *Borderline Citizen* should be required reading for the twenty-first century and beyond."

—XU XI, author of *This Fish Is Fowl: Essays of Being*

"Robin Hemley begins *Borderline Citizen* with the observation that 'as travelers, we see surfaces first. It's easy to exoticize, to misinterpret, nearly impossible to see something except through our own lenses.' He then goes on to show how a thoughtful, perceptive, and openhearted traveler can overcome all those limitations. In vividly rendered essays, Hemley takes us to some of history's oddest bits of territory, showing how human lives are shaped (and often distorted) by arbitrary political boundaries. With superb storytelling, he explores the meanings of nationalism, sovereignty, citizenship and the loyalties of the human heart."

—COREY FLINTOFF, former NPR foreign correspondent

"In these days of ultranationalism comes a surprising antidote in Robin Hemley's cabinet of curiosities, *Borderline Citizen*, his account of his journeys to the 'bits and bobs' of national territories stranded by accidents of geography, history, and stubbornness. Hemley is a delightful guide, but there are serious questions for him to explore here as well—and lessons for all the mainlands and mother countries about the meaning and price of national identity. Quite possibly the most original travel book published in years."

—JEFF SHARLET, author of *The Family* and *This Brilliant Darkness*

BORDERLINE CITIZEN

AMERICAN LIVES   *Series editor:* Tobias Wolff

Borderline
Citizen

DISPATCHES FROM THE OUTSKIRTS OF NATIONHOOD

Robin Hemley

University of Nebraska Press | Lincoln

For the small but ever-changing "nation" ruled by
Margie, Olivia, Isabel, Shoshie, and Naomi, and
for my family and friends across the world

I have never in my life "loved" any people or collective—
neither the German people, nor the French, nor the
American, nor the working class or anything of that sort.
I indeed love "only" my friends and the only kind of love
I know of and believe in is the love of persons.

HANNAH ARENDT

Travel in order to listen to the world
rather than lecture to it.

PICO IYER

CONTENTS

ILLUSTRATIONS

ACKNOWLEDGMENTS

In addition to my favorite traveling companions, my family, I'm deeply thankful for various friends who, despite their own busy and full lives, have long supported my transnational life and my work. These include Nicole Walker, Russell Valentino, Lawrence Reid, Xu Xi, Peter Parsons, Heidi Stalla, Lee Kofman, Peter Bishop, Bonnie Sunstein, Gregory Maertz, Leah Kaminsky, David Carlin, Francesca Rendle-Short, Patrick Madden, Catherine Combe, Diana Chester, Jane Camens, Darryl Whetter, and Sarge Lacuesta. I'm likewise greatly appreciative of the following people for their generous assistance in various ways over the years it's taken me to write this: Jennifer Sahn, Bradford Morrow, Gretchen Head, Malaga Baldi, Alicia Christensen, Courtney Ochsner, Dee Dee DeBartlo, Christina Hidalgo, Suzanne Paola, John Vangundy, Tom Larson, and Antony Dapiran.

Of the people living in the various places I visited in order to write this book, Galen Wood was a gracious host and guide. Suzanne Pinckston, Kandace Harper, Peter Courtney, Carol Clark, Annelle Norman, Fred Culbert, and so many other good people of Point Roberts and Tsawwassen took the time as well to inform me about their communities and the issues facing them. In Stanley, the staff of the *Penguin News* were quite helpful to me, as were many other members of the Falkland Islands community (but not the threatening drunk in the Victory Bar), in particular Adrian Lowe and John Fowler. I'm indebted to Bapi Biswas for smoothing the way and taking me everywhere I needed to go in Cooch Behar, as well as my former student, his daughter, Ritika, for her introduction to her family. Aparna Roy was a godsend as a translator and guide. I'm likewise indebted to the former enclave inhabitants of Cooch Behar, though I doubt they will ever read this—but it's my fragile hope that their lives will improve in their new homes and communities. Nehanda Abiodun was generous to both groups of students I led to Cuba and provided us with a perspective on separation from one's land of birth that is rare to encounter. Thank you to Tom Miller for leading us around Havana and introducing us to Nehanda. Thank you, too, Lian, for your friendly and informative assistance in Havana and throughout Cuba.

The world of exclave and enclave research is rather small and they mostly seem to know one another. I'm glad to know them as well. Brendan Whyte, Assistant Map Curator of the National Library of Australia, supplied me with maps and articles on various exclaves, particularly the former exclaves of Cooch Behar and the Baarles. His article, "Bordering on the Ridiculous: A Comparison of the Baarle and Cooch Behar Enclaves," originally published in the *Globe*, was particularly helpful. Evgeny Vinokurov's book on enclaves, *A Theory of Enclaves*, was invaluable, as was the interview I conducted with him in St. Petersburg. I met Ezequiel Mercau by chance or *bashert* in the Falklands/Malvinas and made great use of his dissertation, "Empire Redux: The Falklands and the End of Greater Britain," as well as his article, "War of the British Worlds: The Anglo-Argentines and the Falklands" in the *Journal of British Studies*. Willem van Gool was the most informative and pleasant companion one could possibly encounter in the Baarles, and I'm grateful not only for his expertise but for his time and energy devoted to helping me with this project.

I would love to be able to thank publicly several people who requested anonymity, but I will just have to leave it at this meager acknowledgment of gratitude.

This project would not have been possible to complete without the generous financial assistance and confidence in me shown by Yale-NUS College in Singapore. I'm indebted to the college and its generous support, and for the equally crucial support of the Ministry of Education of Singapore.

I am also indebted to the following organizations that gave me the space and time to write in places of great beauty and intellectual stimulation: the Bogliasco Foundation where I began this book and the Rockefeller Foundation's Bellagio Center, where I completed it.

Thank you to the various publications that originally published chapters of this book, sometimes in different form.

"The Great Land Swap" and "Mr. Chen's Mountain" were published in *Pacific Standard*.

"Independence Days" and "To the Rainforest Room" were both originally published in *Orion*. "To the Rainforest Room" also appeared in *The Pushcart Prize Anthology*.

"Close Calls with a Potentially Violent Felon in Cuba" was originally published in the *New York Observer*.

"Celebrating Russian Federation Day with Immanuel Kant" originally appeared in *Conjunctions*.

"No One Will See Me Again Forever" originally appeared in *Panorama: The Journal of Intelligent Travel*.

"They Have Forgotten Many Things" originally appeared in the *Iowa Review*.

"Field Notes for the Graveyard Enthusiast" originally appeared in *New Letters*.

"Present" originally appeared in the anthology *Get Lucky* (Ethos Books, Singapore).

"Survivor Stories" originally appeared in *Hunger Mountain*.

"The Traveler in the Twenty-First Century" originally appeared, in somewhat different form, in *Tomás*, the journal of the University of Santo Tomas (Philippines), and in *Text* (Australia).

"Don't Be Too Difficult" originally appeared in *Speak*.

BORDERLINE CITIZEN

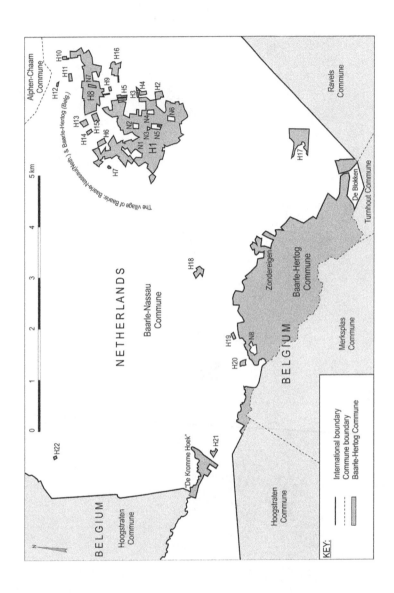

1. The Baarles and environs. Courtesy of Brendan Whyte.

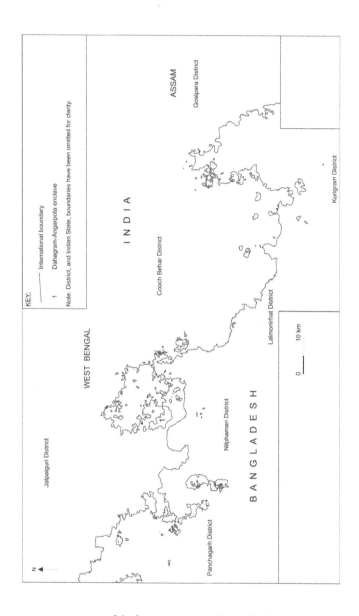

2. A map of the former exclave/enclaves of India and Bangladesh. Note the islands of territory enclaved by both respective nations. Courtesy of Brendan Whyte.

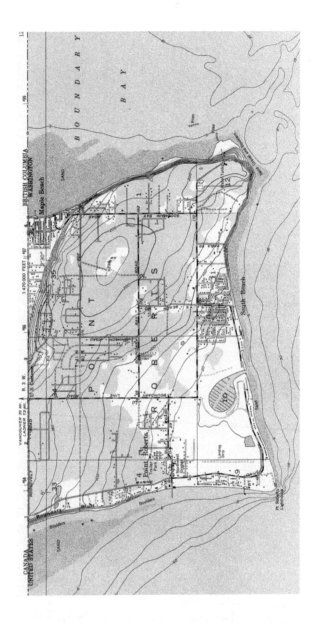

3. The U.S. exclave of Point Roberts. Point Roberts WA. Historical Map.
GEOPDF. Survey Date: 1952. Product Number: 350661. Courtesy of the USGS.

Prologue

The plane from St. Petersburg was in a holding pattern over Moscow, reducing my already short connection time. I could *not* afford to miss my flight to Hong Kong because my Russian visa expired at midnight and it was already past seven in the evening. I'd read horror stories of travelers who'd overstayed their Russian visas by only a couple of hours, and who wound up not only greatly inconvenienced but in trouble. My plane to Hong Kong was due to depart at 8:15 p.m. and, in my state of panic and exasperation at 7:30 p.m. when the plane finally landed, I took every further delay as a personal affront on the part of Aeroflot and whatever bureaucratic under-demon in hell handles the flight itineraries of mortals such as myself. Another fifteen minutes passed as we filed in slow motion out of the plane and onto waiting buses to take us to the terminal. From there, I ran through a hallway that seemed to have been styled after a pneumatic tube, but with none of a pneumatic tube's advantages of propulsion. Huffing along with a fellow passenger to the third floor and passport control—8 p.m. by this time—he remarked as we stepped on the elevator, "This always happens to me." And I had thought it only happened to me.

After passport control, I passed another mile from terminal D to F through another human-scale pneumatic tube and acreage of duty-free shops and restaurants. By the time I reached my gate, it was 8:20 p.m., my mouth parched, my heart racing, my clothes soaked in perspiration. The door to my gate was closed, and a woman on a phone chatted away as though all was right with the world. If one can *forlornly brandish*, then that's how I showed her my ticket. She shrugged and pointed to her left. Behold, an open door and attendants taking such tickets, brandished by my fellow passengers in anything but a forlorn manner. The first attendant who greeted me as I stumbled aboard looked at me as though I were the last survivor of a desert caravan that had been caught in a windstorm and brought me a glass of water.

I collapsed in my seat and thought that my leave-taking of Russia felt under the circumstances more like an escape. Coincidentally, as I was making my way to Hong Kong and then to my new home of Singapore, where I'd recently accepted a job, Edward Snowden was heading to Moscow from Hong Kong. Perhaps we'd pass within miles of one another in the air. Snowden, the infamous, at times celebrated, former NSA employee who had embarrassed the U.S. with allegations of mass spying by the government on millions of Americans as well as allied world leaders, was truly escaping the U.S. He'd spent the last several weeks hiding out in Hong Kong, trying to find a country to take him in while the U.S. pressured Beijing and Hong Kong to hand him over. Public sentiment in both places strongly favored Snowden and so he made good his escape.

Well, Snowden had his life to live and I had mine. We were headed in opposite directions, but we were both turning our backs on our country, though he more dramatically than myself. Putin didn't really want him and kept him holed up in a waiting area of the Moscow airport for weeks before finally welcoming him with folded arms.

The man seated beside me on the plane to Hong Kong, muscular and compactly built, noticed my passport, which I had placed for a moment on my food tray.

"You American?" he asked. "You patriot?"

This is a question that no one had ever asked me before, and I was taken aback. He saw my hesitation and answered first.

"Me, no, not patriot of Ukraine. Bad president, bad police, bad schools. People good. Scenery good. You patriot?" he asked again.

Truthfully and in hindsight, I don't know the answer to that question. I'm not un-American, but I'm not jingoistic by a long shot. I'm not even sure what "American" means anymore. The more I travel, the more I have identity questions, starting with: How American am I? It seemed to me that America and I were both undergoing prolonged identity crises, and now I was moving away, and America, too, seemed to be drifting.

"I guess," I said.

"Passport please," he said as though he were a border guard.

I gave him my passport and asked for his Ukrainian passport. I liked its bright red cover.

"Not so interesting," he said as he handed it over. "Your passport, interesting." As he flipped through my passport, he started to hum "The Star-Spangled Banner," soon rising to a crescendo and looking up with glee from my passport, waving his finger conductor style. "DA DA DA DA DA THAT OUR FLAG DA DA DA."

I introduced myself in a gambit to curtail further singing, if possible. He stopped and said he was Alex from Kiev. Soon, I learned more than I cared to know, in the way that you sometimes do on planes. He loved Ahmadinejad, the Iranian president who insisted the Holocaust never happened, and he disliked Obama because he was "African, not American." He liked Putin.

Happily, after our initial conversation, my Ukrainian friend Alex lost interest in me after he discovered that his favorite movie, *Once Upon a Time in America*, could be viewed on his personal screen. While he watched the movie, I pondered Alex's question more intently than he might have imagined.

What other travelers meditate on is their business, but in my case, the questions I've sought to understand, if not fully answer, are those surrounding nationalism, patriotism, and the almost universal need that people have to belong to some collective or another. I'm in agreement with Hannah Arendt when she writes, "I have never in my life 'loved' any people or collective—neither the German people, nor the French, nor the American, nor the working class or anything of that sort. I indeed love 'only' my friends and the only kind of love I know of and believe in is the love of persons." Like Arendt, I was born without the patriot gene, at least where the loyalty is to a country or an institution. My loyalties are multiple. There are few places I have ventured that I dislike and few people I've met from whom I cannot learn something. I am the person who will gladly talk to my seatmate on a plane (in most cases). I'm interested in your beliefs as long as you don't foist them upon me. I'm curious about what you can tell me about your blind spots and more interested in what you can tell me about my own.

Personally, I like the way the Acadians think of national identity. The Acadians are the descendants of the French settlers in Canada who were ethnically cleansed by the British in the 1700s, the forbearers of today's Louisiana Cajuns. I met an Acadian author, Françoise Enguehard, on Bastille Day on the island of St. Pierre in the North Atlantic, France's last possession in North America. The Acadians no longer have a homeland, but they have everything else that goes with nationality. Enguehard explained to me that "Acadie is an imaginary country that you make up in your heart every day. Not a nationhood of geography and frontiers but of genealogy and common purpose. By being that way, you understand everything that's wrong with nationalism. We have a flag. We have a national anthem. We sing it and we're happy as clams. We have rallied around the symbols of nationhood but we don't have a territory to fight over. It's wonderful. It's freeing. People without a state have something to offer, the higher sense of who we are without all the bullshit." Perhaps the "bullshit" that Enguehard refers to is the notion that any modern nation is more than something imagined every day by its inhabitants, whether in their hearts, their minds, or their land holdings. In 1982, Benedict Anderson, in his book *Imagined Communities*, wrote about the ways in which nations pretend to be ancient, looking toward antiquity for their raison d'être, while actually being quite recent inventions. Nations are imagined and reimagined every day.

On March 11, 1882, a century before Benedict Anderson weighed in on the matter, French philosopher Ernest Renan delivered to a conference at the Sorbonne an essay titled "What Is a Nation?" In some ways, it seems like a simple question, but it's a question that has perplexed and intrigued people since Renan asked it. A hundred years later, Hugh Seton-Watson, the British historian and political scientist, still couldn't answer Renan's question. "I am driven to the conclusion that no 'scientific definition' of the nation can be devised," he wrote, "yet the phenomenon has existed and exists."

If we look at a world map of 1882 we see how different the nations of today look from the days of Renan. In 1882, Germany was eleven years old, Italy twenty-one years old, and India was a compilation of almost six hundred princely states. Australia wouldn't be an independent nation for another nineteen years. Simply put, Renan saw himself ultimately as part of a larger community. "We must not abandon this fundamental principle," he wrote, "that man is a reasonable and moral being before he is penned up in this or that language, a member of this or that race, or a participant in this or that culture. Before French, German, or Italian culture is the culture of mankind."

Given that nations, as we know them today, are something rather new in history, my questions are: What is the nation from which we travel, and what is the nation to which we travel? Who are the twenty-first-century travelers, and how will they record their travels?

Some of them are as well-heeled as any traveler in the past, but some of them are refugees. For me, the complexity of the relationship of the citizen to his or her own nation is the big question of the twenty-first century. Where do we travel simply by consenting to be citizens of the places of our birth? And how do these countries travel beyond us, writing their own travel narratives that bring us along or leave us behind, with or without our consent?

A single lifetime is long enough to have multiple national identities. Mohammed Ali, seventy-nine years old in 2015, was born in British India, and then in 1947 when India and Pakistan went their separate ways, he became a citizen of East Pakistan, an "exclave" (or extra-territorial part of a country cut off from its mainland by another country) of Pakistan; then in 1971, he became a citizen of Bangladesh after East Pakistan fought a war of independence against Pakistan. But for many years, he lived in a Bangladeshi exclave within India. On June 15, 2015, he was given the rare choice of what nationality he wanted to be, along with thousands of other exclave residents on both sides of the Indian-Bangladesh border. Did he want to be Indian or Bangladeshi? June 15 was the date that the two countries swapped their holdings within the countries of the other, simplifying after many decades what had been the most complicated border in the world. At age seventy-nine, Mohammed Ali, a resident of the former Bangladeshi exclave of Bhatrigachh, chose Indian citizenship. "I was born in British India, grew up in East Pakistan and Bangladesh and will spend my old age in India," he told a reporter from the *Gulf Times* in 2015. Mr. Ali is the rarest of travelers of the twenty-first century: a visitor to several countries without moving once.

These identity problems are not simply for the lowly born, like Mohammed Ali, but for monarchs, too.

King Peter II of Yugoslavia and his wife, Alexandra of Greece, faced a dilemma in the summer of 1945 as they awaited the birth of their child, the heir to the throne of Yugoslavia. As with many royals, World War II had scattered them, and the Yugoslavian king and his family had taken up residence in Suite 212 of the Claridge Hotel in London. The problem, besides living in exile, was that the rules of succession stipulated that the heir to the throne had to be born on Yugoslavian soil. This was at a time when the British Empire, even diminished and fraying at the seams, could draw a border or create a nation out of almost nothing. Two years later, Britain would send Sir Cyril Radcliffe to India, a place he had never been, and require that he draw a border between India and Pakistan in little over a month. I imagine Churchill barely blinking, perhaps pausing for a puff on his cigar, before announcing that the problem of the Yugoslavian succession was an easy one: simply declare Suite 212 of the Claridge Hotel temporary Yugoslavian territory on the day of the birth.

When it comes to countries and borders and sovereignty, little is ever that easy. Already in 1945, the communist partisans of Josip Tito had defeated the Nazis and the royalists for control of the country. Less than a month after Crown Prince Alexander's birth, the name of Yugoslavia was changed to Democratic Federal Yugoslavia. By November, the country had changed again, and by 1947 Prince Alexander and virtually his entire family were stripped of their Yugoslavian citizenship, their property confiscated. From the time of his birth until 1991, as Yugoslavia was once again breaking apart and he was finally allowed to visit the country he might have ruled in different circumstances, the only time he ever touched Yugoslavian "soil" was upon his birth, in suite 212 of the Claridge Hotel, an exclave of Yugoslavia for one brief royal moment.

Certainly, the United States that I was born in is no longer the United States I know. It is a country to which I travel warily now, unsure of its consent of me, and unsure of my consent of it. I enjoy celebrating other people's national holidays as much, if not more, than my own, in part because I'm put off by the myopia of so many in my country who have used patriotism and American exceptionalism as smokescreens for a woeful ignorance of the rest of the world. Give me Australia Day or Bastille Day or India's Republic Day, though I will never be a citizen of any of them.

Consent is important here—the consent of one country to receive the traveler, the consent of the traveler to return home, and the consent of his home country to allow him to return. For Renan, the members of a nation, in a metaphorical sense, have a daily plebiscite in which they reaffirm belonging to the nation. Renan knew he was being idealistic when he suggested that land disputes be settled by the inhabitants of those disputed areas. Still, I'm attracted naively to this notion of a citizenry's consent. Is consent something the travel writer should consider writing about? How freely can she move between borders? How difficult is it for the people whose country she visits to travel in the other direction?

The traveler in the twenty-first century might do well to observe the swirl of history and geographies around her, might do well to consider the fragility and complexity of national identity, like Pico Iyer staked out at the international exit of Los Angeles International Airport, observing the homecomings and first visits to the United States of the travelers pouring out the doors, in this way, traveling alongside them, if only for an instant. Granted, Pico Iyer wrote his LAX essay before the twenty-first century, and perhaps the travelers he'd glimpse now would be different, more furtive, warier, more exhausted, or perhaps that's just me projecting my own furtiveness on these hypothetical twenty-first-century travelers.

Inescapably, as travelers, we see surfaces first. It's easy to exoticize, to misinterpret, and nearly impossible to see something except through our own lenses. The traveler in the twenty-first century might do well to recognize his subjectivity, to question his own biases and prejudices, whether conscious or not, might do well to seek to demystify rather than exoticize, and accept that sight is always out of focus, but clearer at least than eyes closed tightly shut. The traveler in the twenty-first century might also be someone from within a culture rather than an outsider, someone who travels without moving an inch, like that wonderful French writer of the eighteenth century, Xavier de Maistre, who under house arrest decided to pass the time by writing a travel narrative from within his confinement, a minor classic still in print titled *Journey Around My Room*.

Anthropologists often throw away the first three months of their notes, but first impressions can be useful, if only as a way to begin to understand the ways in which we move from certainty to uncertainty, from generalization to the particular. The traveler would do well to observe vulnerably, perhaps *should* observe vulnerably, to begin to understand and begin to challenge her own stereotypes and assumptions.

We can't avoid seeing through our cultural lenses, our biases and prejudices, but must we always see the world through the lens of the nations to which we belong? How is the traveler bent to the political will of politicians? Perhaps the better question is how is she not bent to the will of politicians with their aims of solidifying borders rather than permeating them? As a virtue, loyalty to a country or any institution seems overrated and, in some cases, dangerous.

After nearly six years of living in Singapore, I'm not much closer to answers about my own sense of belonging, or where I belong. But I can say this with certainty: leaving my birth country has served as my means of confronting the complexities of my own identity. When I moved, some people asked me how I could give up the "freedoms" of America in order to live in a place without a free press ruled by an "autocratic" government. I moved in 2013, during Obama's presidency and well before Trump's many attacks on the press. Even so, I thought the question suggested a narrow sense of freedom and perhaps a lack of understanding of the degrees of autocracy between a country such as Singapore and another such as North Korea. It's true that there are cameras everywhere in Singapore and you can get the death penalty for drug possession, but on a day-to-day basis, living in Singapore has all the lack of freedom of a luxury golf course. The freedoms I lacked in Singapore did not bother me on a day-to-day basis, though admittedly, I had some moments that required diplomatic tact and precise wording.

Other than a few minor bumps, living in Singapore felt freer than living in America in many ways. I wasn't as free as Singaporeans, who are freer to travel than Americans. They and the Japanese vie year after year for the most valuable passport in the world. But I felt free at least in other valuable ways. Shortly before moving to Singapore, I was in New Haven, Connecticut, staying at a hotel where the doorman insisted I take a taxi instead of walking ten blocks (I love to walk) to a famous pizzeria in New Haven's Little Italy. The neighborhoods around Little Italy were far too dangerous, he assured me. I wasn't sure if this was true or not, but he finally scared me into taking a taxi. In Singapore, my daughters and wife could walk freely any time of day and night and not fear for their safety in the least. A country's freedoms are not based solely on its laws, though the safety of one's family certainly enters into it.

When I left the U.S. for Singapore, I was of course not myself a refugee, forced to flee my country to escape the terror inflicted upon my family by one collective or another. Sometimes, over my long absence, I have felt a bit like an exile, and friends and strangers alike treated me as such, questioning me on the craziness that seemed to have taken over America since the election of 2016. I was just as baffled as they, and I agreed when they told me they thought it was a good time to be outside of the U.S. Still, I was an expatriate, able to choose to a certain extent my place of residence outside of my country and the option always to return. We hadn't sold our home when we moved to Singapore and so it was always there, as were our old friends and our children's friends.

In 2013, I heard a lot about American exceptionalism. I've heard nothing about it recently, except in its crudest form, "America First." Obviously, the world has been troubled of late by the opposite of Arendt's credo, the love of collectives over persons. In my own way, I've sought to examine this phenomenon by traveling to places and meeting people who in some way illustrate some aspect of belonging, nationalism, or patriotism. I've pursued this, in part, by traveling to exclaves, enclaves, and overseas territories, separated from their "motherland," to understand upon what foundations rest the notions of loyalty that make people love their "collective," to the exclusion of all others. My visits have taken me to the exclaves (those bits and bobs of territory of one country surrounded by another country) of Kaliningrad, Russia, for Russian Federation Day; Point Roberts, Washington (for the Fourth of July and Canada Day); and the exclaves of Cooch Behar along the India-Bangladesh border around India's national day. I've visited the Falkland Islands (known as Las Malvinas by Argentina) for Guy Fawkes Day and Hong Kong on Handover Day. I've interviewed Afghan refugees, Indian refugees, a Chinese billionaire, and a fugitive living in Cuba with multiple FBI warrants against her. I've considered the universal citizenship of the graveyard, survivors of Auschwitz, and the bigotries and cultural misunderstandings that lead to bloodshed and environmental degradation in such places as the Philippines and the Ecuadorian rainforest.

On that last point of environmental degradation, there's this: I was asked at a conference several years ago during the Q&A period after a panel presentation on travel writing, whether it was time for travel writers to stop traveling. Given the negative environmental impact of a world in constant motion, the approximately 1.4 billion international tourism arrivals per year (as of 2018, according to the

United Nations World Tourism Organization), degrading the planet by descending upon the world's once most beautiful beach, or a ruined ruin, or a devastated coral reef, the question makes perfect sense. I answered as truthfully as possible: I know, of course, that besides traveling being a privilege of the elite, added to this is the privilege of my skin color. But it seems to me that people who are accustomed to self-interrogation, meditative writers asking difficult questions of themselves and of the world, can offer as much as they take, or at least make the effort to do so. Some writers of place, myself hopefully included, traveling as part of their attempt to understand the complexities of the world, are trying to do so to share something with others that offsets in a generous spirit the harm that's done in the act of travel itself. To some degree, I admit this is a rationalization, but the only way I can make it true is to try to write something of lasting value that will have made my wanderings across the earth worth it to someone else besides me.

Walled Citizens

Through no planning of my own, my landing in Hong Kong coincided with Handover Day, commemorating the return of the former overseas territory of England to China in 1997. My friend Xu Xi and I planned to celebrate the holiday with a bottle of duty-free champagne on the rooftop of her illegally constructed apartment, where we hoped to view the fireworks, after a day of watching the protests of Hong Kong citizens, for whom the handover hadn't turned out quite as they had hoped.

I met Xu Xi at her office the next day and we made our way by taxi to the former Walled City of Kowloon, now an innocuous looking, forgettable park adjacent to a shopping center. But at one time, the Walled City had been the most densely populated place in the world: 6.4 acres that were home to over thirty-three thousand people before the place was demolished in 1994. In the shadow of the old Kai Tak airport, residents of the Walled City had once gone to the rooftops to escape their claustrophobic living conditions and for some fresh air as jumbo jets made their final approach to the runway.

The Walled City began its life as a fort to guard against pirates, and when the British leased the New Territories of Hong Kong in 1898, the Walled City became an exclave of China. The Walled City, outside of British jurisdiction and Chinese control, became a lawless place run by the Chinese Triad gangs. A solid block of high-rises and narrow, shadowy warrens dripping water constantly, not one architect contributed to its construction, and not one regulation or health code could be enforced. Yet people got on with their lives and by no means were they all criminals. By the time it was demolished, the crime rate was relatively low.

The park that was once the Walled City seemed like a good place to begin our day exploring a demolished former exclave within a former overseas territory with identity problems greater than my own. And my friend Xu Xi was the perfect guide and companion on this day. The Hong Kong in which she had grown up in the 1960s was as nonextant as the Walled City itself. In her youth, her apartment had been on the waterfront, but now because of land reclamation, the waterfront was nowhere near her old neighborhood, and the neighborhood itself had mostly been demolished and rebuilt. Born with an Indonesian passport but unable to speak Bahasa, she had similarly slippery notions of national identity as myself. When she was fourteen or fifteen, she read an article about world citizenship and, after researching it, she applied for and received a passport as a world citizen.

"I was an Indonesian citizen and there were a lot of places I had difficulty going. It technically was a passport. There were a few African countries that accepted it. My father never encouraged us to take a British passport even though we probably knew more about Britain than America. All of us wanted to go to America."

A world passport might sound like a scam to separate impressionable kids from their allowance money, but it was actually the brainchild of an intriguing, if idealistic, man named Garry Davis, a former World War II bomber pilot and sometime Broadway actor who, taking a cue from the United Nations charter, had the idea of creating an organization that would sanction global citizenship and even issue passports for these citizens. He even gave up his citizenship in the process. Notables such as Albert Einstein and Albert Camus lauded his efforts and his organization exists to this day. Remarkably, Garry Davis and others have traveled on the World

Passport and at least six countries have officially recognized the passport, while others have done so on a case-by-case basis. It's not easy being a global citizen. Traveling on his world passport, he was imprisoned twenty times at international borders. The first time I had ever heard of him was the day that Xu Xi mentioned him to me, and he passed away at the age of ninety-one only three weeks after I met Xu Xi in Hong Kong, though not before attempting to send Edward Snowden a global passport.

A typhoon was coming in that day; there was no shelter in the now unwalled city; and the wind was picking up. The typhoon warning system was already at Signal 3, steady winds with gusts up to 110 kilometers an hour. After the Walled City, we were going to head to Central to watch the protests against Beijing's increased interference, as the Hong Kong residents saw it, in their affairs. If the warnings reached Signal 8, the protests would be canceled.

"I was always very envious of American citizens," Xu confided as we strolled through the park, more or less oblivious to the gusts as it was still a sunny day. "Americans had the privilege of being idealistic. It was more difficult to be idealistic if you were Indonesian or from Hong Kong."

As the weather quickly worsened, picnickers in the park hurried to gather their things as their blankets threatened to blow away. A group of domestic helpers sought shelter under a flimsy covering as clouds moved in quickly, while Xu and I made a dash to the safety of another walled city: the mall known as Kowloon City Plaza.

Shortly, we found a taxi rank and headed for the protests across the city. When we reached Central, the only people out in force were groups of Filipino domestic helpers who were having picnics as they do every day off, in a fiesta mood, along the walkways of the covered pedestrian overpasses. The streets were otherwise mostly empty as the rain set in, except for riot police and pro-democracy banners calling for the ouster of the Beijing-backed chief executive of Hong Kong. The issue at hand was self-determination. In 1997, Hong Kong had stopped being an overseas territory of the UK, but in the view of Xu Xi and many others, it had simply traded one colonial master in a sense for another. Even Beijing grudgingly recognized its special status with its declared policy of one China, two systems. That sounded good, but clearly Beijing wanted to wean Hong Kong of its specialness. It wasn't and isn't a colony of China. It's part of China. But its history and traditions were different.

"We weren't a nation state," Xu Xi says, "but we wanted to be. I don't think anyone misses the British, but everyone thought it would be okay and it's not as okay as everyone thought."

For Xu Xi, it mattered less. As a naturalized Hong Kong citizen with Indonesian roots, she always felt like an outsider. And she has an "out" as a naturalized American. But her friends, the people she'd grown up with: they're Chinese now. They really *are* Chinese. I have all these local friends who are very proud of being Chinese. And that makes me feel more of an outsider. But even they are feeling dislocated. They didn't expect China to become so wealthy so quick or to become their rulers so quick. I sense an unease now among people who are rooted and loyal in a way that I'm not so rooted and loyal. I readily see myself retiring in America. They don't. Their fate is here. What they didn't anticipate is that Hong Kong would change and become more like China. They want to live here, and here was fine when it was cosmopolitan, but now that's going away.

If they felt dislocated in 2013, how much more dislocated they must have felt a year later with the advent of the Umbrella Movement when thousands took to the streets to protest Beijing's "reforms." The protesters occupied various areas of the city for two months before being ultimately cleared away. Chalk up one (inevitable?) victory for the nation of China, one defeat for the people of Hong Kong, as many saw it. Still, in the lobby of one Hong Kong university I used to frequent, a scale replica stood of the "Goddess of Democracy," a thirty-foot-high statue that had been erected in 1989 in Tiananmen Square before the military moved in and killed hundreds of students on June 4 of that year, a date ignored for the most part by the mainland but tenaciously commemorated by the people of Hong Kong.

And what of Alex, my Ukrainian seatmate on my flight to Hong Kong? Was he still a fan of Putin? Had Alex transformed finally into a patriot? In 2013, I hadn't heard of Paul Manafort, Trump's one-time campaign manager, who traveled to Ukraine to make over another unlikely contender, Viktor Yanukovych, into presidential material, though Yanukovych was widely considered "oafish and inarticulate" and had served time in jail (as Manafort would, too). A year after Alex and I shared a flight, Yanukovych was ousted in a popular revolt, the "Ukrainian Revolution," by thousands of protesters. Seemingly more successful than the Hong Kong protests at first, this particular contest between nations and people ended (for now) in a draw. Shortly after the protesters ousted the Ukrainian president, Russia retaliated by invading and annexing the Crimean Peninsula and supporting Russian separatists in the Donetsk region of Ukraine. In the economy of protest and revolt, identities are snatched away and reclaimed, only to be snatched away again.

In 2019, the protesters in Hong Kong returned in force, two million strong, to oppose Carrie Lam, the chief executive of the territory, who wanted to push through an extradition law that would allow Beijing to clamp down on anyone they see as an enemy. Over the years since the handover, Hong Kong had found a new identity. According to longtime Hong Kong resident, Antony Dapiran, writing in the *Guardian*, the "Core Values" of Hong Kong mean that the people not only have a right but a duty to participate in a meaningful and independent way in their own governance, especially when they see their rights threatened. What does it mean to be a Hong Konger, Dapiran wrote, can be summed up as, "I am a Hong Konger, therefore I protest."

If Hong Kongers were unwilling to see Edward Snowden, that whistleblower-traitor-patriot extradited to the U.S. in 2013, they certainly weren't going to take kindly to the notion of Beijing extraditing their own dissenters in 2019. Carrie Lam and Beijing might have expected as much.

And what of Edward Snowden? To this day, there are plenty of opinions on both sides of the issue, though he sees himself unequivocally as a patriot. Still living in Moscow (at an undisclosed location) he would likely have less trouble than I answering the question that Alex from Ukraine posed to me on my flight from Moscow to Hong Kong in 2013.

All these identity problems were still quite fluid in 2013 as Xu Xi, that would-be global citizen and I, in a festive mood, waited for the protesters to show up. Finally, in the distance, we heard chanting and soon the first protesters appeared as if straggling back from a concert, families and people of all ages walking at a leisurely pace, chatting and laughing. As the marchers came into view, I heard them sing a song that sounded both familiar and unintelligible. "It's from *Les Misérables*," Xu Xi told me. "'Do You Hear the People Sing?' in Cantonese."

No One Will See Me Again Forever

The smugglers said the journey would take twenty-four hours max. The boat that H and the other eighty asylum seekers would travel in was massive, so big that it could not get to the shore, making it necessary for them to be split in two groups and placed on smaller boats that would meet the larger one an hour later. But when they reached the rendezvous spot, H saw the new ship was not massive at all, just a little bigger than the smaller boats that could barely hold forty. The smugglers said, never mind, just get on board. You have no choice. Or just bad choices: drown or get picked up by the Indonesian police and thrown in a cell of twelve people meant for six, where only six would sleep at a time and the rest would stand and watch the others sleep. One of H's companions had experienced one of these cells. The cell almost never saw sunlight; the only glimpse of light was at feeding times when food would be shoved in from a hole in the roof. H had no trouble imagining this cell or making sense of it. His was a problem of space. The little space he took up on earth was already too much. If he lay down for good, if he drowned, if he burned or rotted, turned to dust, his space problem would be solved.

On the second night, H thought they might be arriving because the boat was slowing. But soon he noticed the frightened expressions of the crew and saw them trying to fix the engine. That night, the wind-driven waves smashed into the boat. His thoughts were louder than sobs and shouts, than waves as they cracked over the deck. He couldn't swim and he saw himself die a hundred times that night, his last thoughts of his mother as the water filled the empty spaces in his lungs.

By the second night, the crew still hadn't fixed the engine and the boat continued to drift.

By the third night, they had no idea where they were and water covered everything. In one spot the whole time, he couldn't move, he couldn't eat, and he couldn't sleep. He just kept thinking, "How will I die? How will I die?" This track wore a groove into his mind so deep his terror would never be able to scale the canyon walls and leave him. He approached the thought, "I don't swim," as though it were a math problem, something to study that might be solved with logic or clarity of mind. But he had no clarity, and the thought that he couldn't swim was unsolvable, as was the larger problem that he would never see his family again. He was only seventeen and this was the first time he'd been separated from them.

On the fifth day, they were rescued by the Australian navy. That was three years ago. Now this thin young man in the checkered shirt and glasses sits across from you and your daughter in a restaurant in Sydney, Australia. As she listens to him, she sits expressionless and still, but in her eyes there is an almost visible reflection of the waters in which H nearly perished. "We were lucky," H says, then takes a sip of tea, his tone not one of happiness but of weariness, too much weariness for someone as young as he is.

Every night, he's drowning. He's sinking. Or the Taliban are after him. He sleeps three hours at best—if only he could get by on no sleep . . . His cries wake his housemates, and one of them places a hand on his trembling shoulder, or his head, wooing him back from the depths of the deaths that might have been, that still might be in his future. He's lived in this begrudging country for three years, but any day he can be sent back. One day, he received a call and was told never to talk to "the media" about his experiences, but he believes that someone should tell the stories of people like him. He has to do something positive with each day or else there's nothing to live for. His father, a doctor who saved hundreds of lives, the first in his Hazara community, told him to go to school and give back to the community. It doesn't matter what community as long as it's a human being.

Most days, he doesn't think about the future because he believes he has none. When he calls his mother, he's not just saying hello. "Imagine your family is in a war zone and you can't do anything to protect them." Last month, his younger brother was beaten. There's no more money to send his brother to join him, and even if she could somehow spirit him out of Afghanistan, he wouldn't even be as fortunate as H. If he didn't drown at sea, the authorities would bring him to the barren island nation of Nauru off Australia's northern coast, where they're sticking all refugees now who arrive by sea, vowing never to let them settle here.

He does what he can to help asylum seekers like himself: reading letters, filling out forms, teaching computer literacy one night a week. He received a call about a family in the refugee camp with two high school age girls who, every morning, were escorted by guards to school and, every afternoon, escorted back. He couldn't stop crying for thirty minutes when he met them. They didn't do anything wrong. They're just human beings. They just came here to seek protection. Is that too much to ask? Now they want to go to university. H and some others were able to secure a scholarship for them at the University of Western Sydney where they will be escorted back and forth from school in the same manner, as though they are criminals.

"Mentally we are not safe," H tells you and your daughter. He knew a man who poured petrol on himself and set himself on fire.

Another friend's entire family died in the same instant in a bomb blast.

When he first arrived, he knew no English, but now he speaks fluently with a soft Aussie accent, perhaps the only permanent residue this country will leave on him if he's sent away—that and the education he received thanks to some compassionate people at a local college. When he graduated, he called up his mother while he was wearing his graduation robes. "Can you believe it?" he said. "I'm wearing the clothes." His brother had wanted to wear the clothes of graduation, but in his second year at university, the Taliban stopped the car in which he was a passenger, took him from the car, and executed him on the side of the road for being Hazara. His father had wanted to see his sons wear the clothes, but he, too, was taken away by the Taliban and murdered. A year ago, an uncle was murdered. Two months ago, a cousin.

"Is there any way this might change?" you ask him because you're used to solutions to problems. You have grown up believing in positive outcomes.

H closes his eyes and is silent. You can see that he is trying not to break down.

He says, "It's like I have a cancer. I don't have a chance to say how long I'm living. I don't have a voice. The moment I go to the media, I'm gone. No one will see me again forever. The day I land in Afghanistan, I'm dead. But I'm trying to do good before I die. I can't go anywhere else. I have no travel document. I can't see a normal goal like a normal human being. My short goal when I wake up in the morning, I think, let's do something today. At the end of the day, we're all human. We don't have to scare from each other. You have to sit with someone to listen. Just to sit as a human being and listen."

A part of you doesn't want to listen because, well, it's difficult, you have your own problems, and how is this going to affect your daughter? You're not sure she can take any more of his story. You're not sure if you can. H has no choice but to listen to his own story as he tells it.

"How do you feel about Afghanistan?" you ask.

"I love Afghanistan. It's my country."

This is not the answer you expected. How can you love a country that wants you dead, that persecutes you and everyone of your kind? He perhaps doesn't notice the shock in your eyes and continues in his patient voice.

"I belong to that part of the world. But I don't like it. Every day of my life, it's been war. I didn't have a single day to be happy, to enjoy. Every single day there was discrimination. I'm tired of that community. I'm tired of the land. I don't have a single good memory of . . . *that day was so beautiful*. That land took my friends, my family."

Then how, you ask, can you say you love it?

"I love it because of my family. I spent a lot of time in a particular house, with a particular people. If my family wasn't in Afghanistan, I would never go back, not for a day, not for a single moment."

Isn't it strange, you think, that our first reaction is to say we love our countries, when what we love is much less abstract than a nation? You love, for instance, the person sitting beside you. You will always be loyal to her. People do not have their own flags, their own colors, their national bird or national flower. They do not have anthems or pledges. Their borders are as physical as their bodies and as lasting as their mortal lives. Our loyalty to the people we love is so much simpler at the same time it is so much more complex than our love for our nations. You ask this person beside you, this exclave of yourself, if she has any questions for H. Yes, she does. She wants to know if there's anywhere in Sydney, any special place that he likes to go. At first, he doesn't know what to make of the question, and you're not entirely sure either. It's only when you excuse yourself to visit the washroom that he talks to her and tells her how fortunate she is to have a father. Yes, there is a place he likes to visit, she reports to you later. His favorite place in Sydney is the Opera House, where he likes to sit and look out at the sea. His friends think that's strange because he has nightmares about the sea, but he wants to look at the sea because it's endless and he likes to imagine his life that way.

You ask him when his birthday is, not because you want to know his sign, or know when to give him a present, but because you want to know how close he is in age to your daughter. Their lives are so different from one another, but you think that they are probably quite close in age.

Even this is a difficult question. When he was rescued by the Australian navy, he was taken to Christmas Island for processing, where his interrogators insisted that he was eighteen, not seventeen. Eighteen meant he was just another refugee. Seventeen meant he had to be looked after. Seventeen meant they'd have to send him to school, adding to his problem of taking up too much space the problem of being too young. His fake birthday, the one his interrogators gave him, is December 31. His real birthday, you learn, makes him eleven days older than your daughter.

Several weeks later, you'll read in the *Guardian* of a Hazara man who has lost his appeal and will be deported from Australia within a week or so. The papers don't give his name because he fears that if the Taliban learn it, they'll look for him and kill him upon his return. This man, you learn with guilty relief, is twice H's age. The article states that the Australian government considers the violence faced by the Hazaras similar to that faced by other ethnic minorities. Nothing special. Just the usual massacres, beheadings, summary executions, and torture.

After you part with H, you and your daughter walk back to the hotel, at first stunned silent, but then talking almost faster than you can think, as though recounting some near-death experience of your own. Under the circumstances, your walk home feels more like an escape. You tell each other your lives have been changed by this encounter with H, but have they? These tragedies seem as endless as the oceans that would drown us.

The Great Land Swap

Fenced off from neighboring potato and tobacco fields, Mekhli-ganj resettlement camp seemed an anomaly in modern-day India, a mini throwback to the massive refugee crisis that had greeted the country's founding in 1947. Just inside the perimeter of the camp, a mustachioed police officer in leather jacket and blue beret approached me and inquired about my purpose. I was there with permission from the district magistrate of Cooch Behar to interview the former residents of the chhitmahals, I told him, and he asked me to wait while he stepped into his office to make a call to the subdivision office to check this out.

The temperature was still in the fifties, but the morning sun had succeeded in burning off the fog that had accompanied my Bengali translator, Aparna Roy, and me on our two-hour journey from the city of Jalpaiguri. Aparna, like the officer, was dressed for winter, in a black jacket, jeans, and sunglasses. While we waited for the officer to return, we observed a group of teenage boys playing carrom, a game like air hockey, on a homemade table. A sari-clad woman tended to a small field of sticks of rolled cow dung, used as cooking fuel, bundling the ones that had baked in the sun and stacking them by a bamboo bench. A chicken, followed by four chicks, pecked nearby. If not for the corrugated metal barracks, we might have been witnessing village life almost anywhere in India, Bangladesh, or Pakistan, much as it had carried on for centuries.

But life for the forty-eight families in the resettlement camp was anything but typical. Six weeks earlier, in November 2015, the forty-eight families sheltered here had moved from a contingent existence in Bangladesh, where they and their ancestors had been marooned as Indian citizens for generations. In August of that year, India and Bangladesh, which share the fifth-longest international border in the world, had swapped 111 Indian districts located within Bangladesh for 51 Bangladesh districts located inside of India.

These incongruous plots of land within the borders of another nation's territory, known geographically as exclaves (or enclaves) and locally as chhitmahals, had been home to approximately fifty-three thousand people, according to a 2011 Indian census—thirty-eight thousand Indians in the exclaves of Bangladesh and fifteen thousand Bangladeshis in the exclaves in India. (An easy, if overly simplistic, explanation is that enclave is to exclave as immigrant is to emigrant: the chhitmahals of India and Bangladesh were both enclave and exclave, in the same way that an immigrant to one country is also an emigrant from another. But also: an exclave is a bit of a country split from its motherland by one or more countries, such as Kaliningrad, Russia, which is separated from Russia by Poland and Lithuania, while an enclave is a territory wholly embedded within another. Only three "true" enclaved nations exist in the world: Lesotho, Vatican City, and San Marino.)

The exclaves exchanged were mostly found along the northernmost part of Bangladesh and along a narrow arm of Eastern India in West Bengal, itself sandwiched between Nepal, Bhutan, and Bangladesh. Twenty-one counter-exclaves existed within these exclaves, and were likewise redesignated in the swap, as was the world's only counter-counter exclave, Dahala Khagrabari, a smidgeon of Indian farmland fewer than two acres in size owned by a Bangladeshi jute farmer. This odd patch of Indian territory was itself surrounded by a Bangladeshi village, which was encircled by an Indian village, which was surrounded by a district within Bangladesh proper. But this wasn't the smallest of the chhitmahals—the exclave earning that distinction consisted of little more than a hundredth of an acre (less than five hundred square feet).

The popular origin story for these absurd bits of territory has the Maharaja of Cooch Behar and the Faujdar of Rangpur putting up as bets in chess games small chits of their territories. Over the years, the modern nations that exist today grew up around their wins and losses. Whenever the two men played, they'd put up a village as one of their stakes. Out of their gambling emerged a patchwork of territories, enveloped within one another like Russian nesting dolls.

Alas, this story has turned out to be the historical equivalent of fake news. The chhitmahals actually came about as the result of a peace treaty in 1713 between the kingdom of Cooch Behar and the declining Mughal Empire, whereby Cooch Behar ceded some of its districts to the Mughals. These lands were not necessarily contiguous or compact, and there were small pockets of territory embedded within the traded districts. Before the advent of modern nations, passports, and tightly regulated borders, such messy alliances and sub-alliances had little impact on people's daily lives. When British India absorbed both kingdoms, the exclaves mattered even less. Only when Britain moved out of the neighborhood, and Pakistan and India were created, did they become a problem.

A rabbit hole of explanations would be required to illuminate the intricate thread of land disputes that occurred in the region in between the hasty and bloody partition of India and Pakistan in 1947, and the political conditions that finally made the swap of the exclaves possible in 2015. But let's give it a try: first, a lawyer who had never set foot in India, Cyril John Radcliffe, was given the task of drawing a border between India and Pakistan in five weeks' time. He inadvertently omitted from the map a police station that should have belonged to India. But its omission from both his map and written report allowed Pakistan a claim. The trouble caused by this one police station wasn't even partially resolved until the 1958 signing of the Nehru-Noon Agreement between the two countries, which was then, predictably, held up in courts until 1971, but then war broke out and East Pakistan was transformed in the conflict into the independent country of Bangladesh. Another land boundary agreement was reached in 1974 between India and Bangladesh that addressed additional "adverse possessions," including the exclaves, which, the two nations agreed, ought to be exchanged. Politics, both local and national, made the agreement's implementation difficult. To some Indian nationalists, Bangladesh was getting the better deal: 17,160.63 acres would be ceded to Bangladesh versus 7,110.02 acres to India. Bangladesh ratified the agreement in 1974, but it took India another forty-one years to approve the swap, largely because of domestic opposition. In 2011, a new protocol was reached resolving the outstanding border issues, but still no time frame was established for implementation. The inertia over the matter was finally over-come when Narendra Modi became prime minister in 2014, and his party introduced a constitutional amendment to force the issue and resolve the dispute once and for all. Only a nationalist party such as a Modi's could have possessed the political capital to thwart the nationalists who opposed the settlement of this issue, it seems.

When I visited the Mekhliganj resettlement camp, one of three such camps set up for the Indian refugees from Bangladesh, in January 2016, I wondered why, out of thirty-eight thousand people, only around nine hundred or so had chosen to uproot their lives in order to retain the Indian citizenship that had been their fragile birthright in the chhitmahals. Their ancestors had been loaded onto this par-ticular runaway train during the British Raj, survived the upheavals of the Partition, the bloody births of East Pakistan and Bangladesh, and now, finally, here they were, waiting in a resettlement camp after being told they could obtain all of the rights and privileges of

Indian citizenship in exchange for leaving the only land they had ever known. Mind the gap.

After checking out my credentials, the mustachioed policeman led Aparna and me among the barracks. He had only worked at the camp for a few days, but he thought the refugees were "happy here." A young civic volunteer, Ersad Ali, who had been at the camp for a month, said that when the refugees first arrived they were traumatized and barely talked. Now they had bonded, but there were obviously many problems for them in their new temporary home. A plastic stool was brought for me, and a hundred men and women crowded around to share their stories.

I asked why they had wanted to move. "We love India," eighteen-year-old Ranajit Roy said. They'd been here since November, and while not everything happened fast enough, they were slowly being integrated into Indian society—Ranajit had been attending an Indian school for the past three days.

"We love India" I took to mean something else, as I wasn't sure I believed in love for a place they had only known in name. Their neighbors in Bangladesh had certainly not loved them, as made clear by the range of atrocities committed against them over the years in the chhitmahals. A woman in a purple sari, fifty-year-old Swapnarani Roy, told of being "ill-treated and rudely tortured," people in the exclave beaten up, houses broken into, burned, Hindus forced to eat beef "to convert them," her husband threatened with murder. "They tried to molest her thirteen-year-old daughter," Aparna told me. Her husband had escaped the exclave with only his life. Lifting up her sari, the woman displayed scars she said were the result of a machete attack.

Sixty-four-year-old Nagendra Barman told of being beaten, his house burned. There were no basic facilities, no law and order. He and others told of "waves of violence" from the beginning, meaning,

I assumed, from Independence, though he was not quite old enough to have lived through that.

When asked whether there were others left behind in the exclaves who would like to follow, a man shouted out and others grew agitated. A woman in her thirties with her arms crossed, Pratima Rani Barman, said more than 2,000 people would come if they were allowed. "There are many places the government didn't go to talk to the residents," she said. The Indian press had reported much the same, one article claiming that the exclave dwellers in Bangladesh had been threatened, and told they shouldn't go to India, the Bangladeshi officials afraid of a "mass exodus" that would represent an enormous "loss of face." While the Indian government has claimed that most residents didn't want to move, the Indian press reported something quite different: Upwards of 13,000 exclave inhabitants in Bangladesh had been expected to move to India after the swap, yet only 2.6 percent of the approximately 38,000 Indian exclave inhabitants, or 987, chose (or were allowed), to do so in the end. A *Times of India* blogger reported in 2015 that many of the exclave dwellers had been overlooked in the 2011 government survey, and that the group Jamaat-e-Islami had "threatened and intimidated" those who wanted to opt for Indian citizenship. "In stark contrast," the blogger asserted, "all of the 14,854 people staying on Indian soil in Bangladeshi enclaves have sought Indian citizenship." At least 2,000 residents stranded in the chhitmahals of India, now Bangladesh, had applied for Indian citizenship after the deadline.

These complaints, while difficult to prove, afford a plausible reason why so few had chosen to move from Bangladesh to India. If life was as hard as they claimed in the chhitmahals—robbed from and beaten, their houses set alight, their daughters molested—then were those left behind loyal, finally, to the land on which they were born and raised, willing to endure hardships to stay with the familiar? Now that they were officially Bangladeshi instead of Indian, and the exclaves in which they had previously lived mooted, would their neighbors treat them any differently?

Due to visa restrictions, I was unable to visit the other side of the border, but I did spend time in all three Indian resettlement camps and heard similar stories of mistreatment in each of them. The big revelation (for me) was that not all the refugees from Bangladesh were Hindu. Out of fifty-five families in the Dinhata resettlement camp, thirty were Muslim. So, it wasn't a simple matter of Hindu versus Muslim. The residents of the chhitmahals had been made to feel inferior to their neighbors by dint of where they lived and how they identified nationally. The hatred exhibited toward them was as arbitrary, as such hatreds almost always are, just more obviously so. Their resettlement had nothing to do with religion, they said. Mijanor Rahman, a Muslim man in his thirties, said that the authorities tried to discourage them from leaving Bangladesh, claiming they would be forced to change their faith upon arriving in India. But after two months at the camp, he said he felt no threat.

Certainly, some settlers were migrating to India for economic reasons, but many of them claimed to own land in Bangladesh, for which they had ancient deeds dating back to the days of the Raj. Another man in his thirties, Mrinal Barman, said it was difficult to sell their land. They had buyers, but the stamps from the authorities needed to finalize the sale were not forthcoming, as the deeds shuttled from one government office to the next. He couldn't collect money from the buyers either. This particular frustration was widespread among those in the resettlement camps, as they were not allowed to travel back to Bangladesh to complete their sales, though some held out hope that at some point they'd be able to return for this purpose.

"The people knew we were leaving," Rahman said. "They'd get the land eventually."

A thirty-minute drive from the Mekhliganj resettlement camp, Dhabalsati Mirgipur, a tiny village of split bamboo and tin roofs, looked no different from the rest of the Indian countryside. Before the exchange of territories, it was officially part of Bangladesh. Electric poles had been erected by the government not long after the swap, I was told, as Aparna and I sat in a small shelter that had also recently been erected. A road bisected the community. On the far side, three banana trees in a field had marked the former border between India and Bangladesh. Behind the shelter, a wide dirt path led into the heart of the village, tobacco fields on one side and huts crowding the other side. There was no actual border visible to anyone here besides locals, who knew that one hut was part of the former Bangladesh enclave and the one farther down the path had always been Indian. Thirty-eight families lived in this former exclave, and it seemed that about half of the men in the village, most dressed in sweater vests and sandals, had crowded around us.

A man named Bipul Chaudhury, in his forties, said that while they had previously been officially Bangladeshi, they had no citizenship papers, so they used to illegally acquire Indian papers. Gautam Adhikary, in his late twenties, had been able to study in India, but had required forged documents to do so. Most of the village had lacked basic services. A few lucky ones, like Gautam, who lived near the road, had been able to hook up connections illegally. As a small community, they tended to sort out their differences among themselves. They developed "understandings." Their village elders took the role of arbiters, though sometimes they asked the head of the Indian village next door to arbitrate. They sometimes had difficulty voting because it was well known locally that they were Bangladeshis. How did they identify? As Indian, Gautam said. "If we can study in Indian schools, run on Indian roads, why should we consider ourselves anything else?"

In Balapukhari, another former exclave, we were told much the same story. A man wearing a T-shirt with names of world cities and a gray skirt-like lungi, Poritosh Roy, said that his family had lived there for generations. When I asked him if he ever considered himself Bangladeshi, his response was a quick and violent, "Nah." The main problems here, he said, were land transactions, as there was no legal documentation. Land titles were ancient, informally arranged among enclave residents, or nonexistent. To create legal documents would have taken years, as he would have had no way to reach Bangladesh to file them. So, the people of Balapukhari had made these transactions ad hoc within the community. While a young woman, a university student, tried to figure out how many generations her family had lived in the former enclave, a man on a bicycle stopped upon seeing the crowd and proclaimed his pride to be Indian. "A lot of people have passed away who would have wished for this day," he said.

The land boundary agreement of 2011 concerned not only the exclaves but other adverse possessions, including that pesky police station in South Berubari that Cyril John Radcliffe had inadvertently omitted from his report. The two countries had created a de facto solution to that situation after the 1974 agreement, which the more comprehensive 2011 agreement formalized. India was allowed to keep the Berubari district intact, police station and all, in exchange for a corridor connecting the rest of Bangladesh to its relatively wealthy and large exclave of Dahagram-Angarpota. The narrow land bridge, known as the Tin Bigha Corridor, has the feel of a heavily fortified municipal park, replete with commemorative plantings and plaques proclaiming Indian-Bangladesh friendship, and guards of both nations posted at the gates. When I visited, a turbaned Punjabi guard was stationed at one end and a Bangladeshi guard at the other. A Bengali friend of mine suggested that the border around the corridor, with its fifteen-foot-high fences, was like North and South Korea, while other parts of the border were like the Netherlands.

Historically, the India-Bangladesh border around Cooch Behar has been relatively porous, with foot traffic moving more or less unimpeded, as I found out after stepping over the border for a quick photo-op a few kilometers away from the Tin Bigha. A local farmer nearly photobombed me as he traipsed from the Indian roadside into a Bangladeshi potato field, the border marked only by a stone pillar the size of a torpedo with India on one side and Bangla on the other.

As Aparna and I traveled on to Berubari, the land bore no obvious scars of its contentious past. The only inconveniences we faced were the occasional dog or goat crossing the road in front of us, dealt with efficiently by our driver with a quick blast of the horn. A salesman on a bike with a bundle of tin cooking utensils set a dreamy pace for us past overarching banyan trees, conical hills of hay, and the occasional tea garden, the road wide enough for only one car. A blue high school building with whitewashed trees set against drab concrete blocks was the only structure of consequence besides a humble mosque, and then virtually nothing but fields fringed with trees, a landscape that looked anything but adverse. A tent of red, yellow, and blue sat alone in a field, and Aparna informed me that the past few days had been auspicious for weddings.

In 1971, this quiet country lane would probably have been clogged with tanks, infantry, refugees, and destruction everywhere. No wedding tents. Or peddlers pedaling their bikes. A nearby Hindu temple, Tristrota Shakti Peeth, destroyed in the fighting, was later rebuilt. Aparna's own family had moved to India when their land in what was then East Pakistan was confiscated.

At a makeshift roadside store, we met a man in his fifties, Gokul Mohanta, who told us that he'd always lived in South Berubari, even when it was Bangladesh. Though it officially became Indian on August 1, 2015, the area had been Indian in every way, except on the map, since 1971—the residents even had Indian voter ID cards, he told us.

But now that the swap was official, the Indian government was wasting no time: along the Berubari border, 10 major pillars and 110 subsidiary pillars were being installed. At that time, the idea wasn't necessarily to construct a barricade, but only to demarcate the line before anyone changed their mind. As if on cue, Biswojit Das, a local resident and engineer working on installing pillars for the new border, pulled up on his motorcycle and joined our conversation. He invited Aparna and me to follow him to his worksite. Carrying a border post, he set a lively pace as we traipsed along a bamboo-lined dirt path raised above a mustard field, a cluster of huts, an old man burning straw, and a cow tied near the path that eyed us warily as we passed. "There," he said, pointing to a copse of trees a cricket pitch's distance ahead. The tea garden near the trees was Indian, while Bangladesh was on the other side. This was a resting place for the Border Security Forces, he told me. I was headed off in that direction when I caught sight from the corner of my eye of an Indian soldier with a gun striding toward me at a brisk pace.

The man asked me to follow him across a field toward a group of men setting pillars. I was soon surrounded by ten other armed men. A short distance away was a group of brown-uniformed Bangladesh border guards eyeing me with what seemed a menacing curiosity. A man in a black leather jacket and aviator glasses separated himself from the Indian soldiers and introduced himself as Kaushik from the Survey of India. He seemed more concerned that I had never heard of the Survey of India than with my trespass on a sensitive border, so I feigned an intense interest in the venerable organization, from its founding in 1767 to its distinction of having designed the first postage stamp in India in 1854, as if my freedom depended on it, which perhaps it did. We posed for a photo together, facing away from the border, which he then invited me to step over. The Bangladesh security forces, meanwhile, hadn't taken their eyes off me, and I imagined all sorts of scenarios.

"Don't worry, sir," he said. "If they wanted to shoot you, you would be dead already."

White privilege and my obvious foreignness had most likely spared me, but more than nine hundred Bangladeshis had been shot by India's Border Security Force between 2001 and 2010, according to a Human Rights Watch report. Returning from India to her father's birth village in Bangladesh in 2011, fifteen-year-old Felani Khatun screamed out when her clothing became entangled in a barbed wire fence. Indian Border Security soldiers opened fire on her and her father, killing her. Photos of her body dangling upside down from the border fence, where the Border Security Forces left her for a day, shocked the region and invited worldwide condemnation.

Crossing the border where I had would probably be quite difficult now, even for a white guy like me. By March of 2017, 50 percent of the Bangladesh-India border had been fenced, with a goal of completion by 2019. In West Bengal, where much of the border is riverine, the Indian government is investing in high-tech surveillance as well as old-fashioned barbed wire.

Governments are necessary, and it's natural to want to consider oneself a part of something larger. But I've never been fully convinced that nations as such make sense, and the story of the exclaves seemed to me the most extreme example of the arbitrariness of borders. And yet the people of the chhitmahals, who were essentially stateless and without rights prior to the land swap, are undoubtedly better off in some important regards. In the resettlement camps, the former residents of the Indian exclaves were given Indian ID cards, as well as a job card that entitled them to a hundred days of government manual work, such as digging ditches—per family, though they had been under the impression the cards were per person. The tin shelters, they complained, were too hot or too cold. These were issues they hadn't anticipated, Mijanor Rahman told me. "Even so, this is 1 percent of what we suffered [in Bangladesh]," he said. Still, the complaints were nearly universal.

Another Muslim man in his thirties, Osman Gani, who sold medicine in Bangladesh, said that the rations provided by the Indian government were not enough—the same rations were doled out to a family of five and a family of two. Rations meant for a month ran out in ten days, and he didn't know where his family's next meal was coming from.

By sheer coincidence, the day I left India my travel happened to coincide with India Republic Day. Small stands along the way were selling Indian flags, and at the airport, military personnel stood in formation as a band played patriotic tunes. In the terminal, all the TVs were tuned to the Republic Day celebrations and, as if anyone around could possibly tune them out as it was, an airport official turned up the volume on the TVs around me full blast. If the refugees in the camps were tuning in on a TV or a radio, perhaps this day of celebration, their first outside of the exclaves—the jets flying over, the bands, the speeches, the soldiers marching—represented to them the voicing of a national promise. Or perhaps it was just like any other uncertain day.

Two years on, the bloom of Indian citizenship had faded for many, as virtually all of the refugees still remained in the temporary camps. With their land unsold in Bangladesh, they had little money at hand, nowhere to go, and few ways to earn money. In August of 2017, an Indian newspaper story about the Dinhata resettlement camp quoted Osman Gani as being completely disillusioned and wanting to return to Bangladesh.

The slippery nature of land ownership, internationally and privately, has continued to haunt residents of both the Indian and Bangladeshi chhitmahals long after the exchange. New infrastructure projects by the Indian government have wreaked havoc in the eyes of some residents of the former exclaves. The Indian press reported not long after my visit that roads were being planned that ran through houses, and that police stations and post offices were being set up on private property. The former enclave residents were receiving a crash course on the realities of citizenship: governments solve some problems and create new ones. As it turned out for the former residents of the chhitmahals, citizenship as a concept made sense, but once the larger deal was struck between states, they had been left in a kind of limbo, stranded between wishful thinking and the realities of global and local politics.

4. House with two house numbers, the Baarles. Courtesy of Tourism Baarle.

Don't Be Too Difficult

At the restaurant Eetcafé De Lantaern, two signs pointing in opposite directions announce, for anyone who's interested, "Nederland, 108 meters," and "Nederland, 212 meters." I'm the only one who seems interested at the moment. Everyone else here, mostly middle-aged, huddled in conversation around media devices and beer, cigar and cigarette smells wafting around them, don't have to look up at a sign to know they're in a pocket of Belgium enclaved by the Netherlands. As I eat herring and drink a beer at one of the tables set up in the street, a band at a nearby stage doesn't seem to care either, as they cycle through a couple of songs from my homeland, the ironic "America" from *West Side Story*, and the earnest "This Land is Your Land," followed by Abba's "Waterloo," named after a famous battle that halted an empire in its tracks, a little over an hour's drive from here. Just in case I don't know where I am, Vodaphone chimes in with an alert: "Welcome to Belgium."

I had originally hoped to visit Baarle-Nassau and Baarle-Hertog during the national holiday of either the Netherlands (April 27) or Belgium (July 21) but instead I've arrived by coincidence on the afternoon of the towns' midsummer festival (July 7), which seems to me now a lucky coincidence to reach this strange town on this day of a localized celebration of unity.

Perhaps the most unusual border town in the world, in and around the Baarles, there are twenty-two pieces of Belgium situated in the Netherlands and seven pieces of the Netherlands lying within Belgian exclaves, making them counter exclaves. A solitary Dutch exclave lies across the greater Belgium border, several kilometers away from where I sit. Like the ex-exclaves on the border of Bangladesh and India, the Baarles formed as a result of feudal agreements that, over time, cemented into side pockets of nationhood. In 1198, two related neighbors who were also royals, Henry I, Duke of Brabant, and Godfrey, Lord of Breda, entered into a complex land exchange. Godfrey, who claimed the town of Baarle, gave his lands to Henry, who then loaned them back to Godfrey as fiefs, essentially making Henry Godfrey's lord. In return, Henry gave Godfrey additional uncultivated lands around Baarle, keeping the cultivated ones for himself so he could collect land taxes on them. Godfrey's lands eventually wound up in the hands of the Dutch Monarchy, the House of Orange, while Henry's lands became known as Baarle onder den Hertog, translated as "Baarle under the Duke," eventually shortened simply to Baarle-Hertog. Over the centuries, none of this was particularly problematic. Like an heirloom set of candelabras, the Baarles were passed down to the Burgundys, then the Austrian Hapsburgs, then the Spanish Hapsburgs, At the end of the Thirty Years' War in 1648, the Baarles were separated—Baarle-Nassau going to the newly independent United Provinces while Baarle-Hertog went to the Spanish Netherlands. In 1713, the Spanish Netherlands became the Austrian Netherlands and then in 1793, revolutionary France annexed them both. At the end of the Napoleonic Wars in 1815, the Austrian Netherlands were incorporated into the larger Kingdom of the Netherlands, including the Baarles, though they were considered part of two different provinces. Like East Pakistan becoming the new country of Bangladesh, a civil war created in 1830 the new country of Belgium, and once again the Baarles were on two sides of an international border.

This village of 8,600 Dutch and 2,600 Belgians is in no other way remarkable, its remarkability entirely man-made, an accident of historical agreement that Henry and Godfrey never could have foreseen. Neither would they have imagined nations as we know them now, our loyalties to lords, counts, and dukes replaced by allegiances to flags, anthems, sports teams, and political parties. Here, perhaps it's more difficult than most places to keep those allegiances straight and uncomplicated. A simple walk through town has one crossing the international border multiple times, often marked on the sidewalks by x's, the flags flying from various buildings, and the address plates on the doors depicting either Belgian or Dutch flags. The international border runs through the front door of one home that consequently has two address plates and two doorbells as well. There are two of everything here: two mayors, two police chiefs, two fire stations, two post offices, two hospitals, two city councils, two schools.

But there's one celebration today. Since my arrival, this town has filled up with hundreds, if not thousands, of people in attendance. It's not so much fun to be a solitary soul in a crowd of revelers you don't know, so after my herring and beer, I make my way back to the place I'm staying, the Hotel Brasserie den Engel. A relief of a smuggler leading a cow graces the wall of the building, a decorative testament to the town's often colorful history. Unlike the exclaves of Cooch Behar, the enclaves of the Baarles have brought prosperity to the town, first through smuggling and later through tourism. For that reason, in large part, a number of the attempts to swap territories at an international level were heartily resisted by the towns' citizens. To get rid of the borders here would be to solve a problem that doesn't need solving and transform the town into just another ordinary village near a border.

It's after eleven, but the square in front of my hotel is still packed with several hundred revelers. A middle-aged man in a pink suit sings Dutch favorites as three policemen dance a funny minuet with a young woman to the delight of those around them. A woman dressed like a stork walks on stilts, flapping her wings as she makes her way through the crowd. A man in a green wig and psychedelic suit follows her. Three teen boys amble in front of me. One drops his beer, stumbling forward like a wounded infantryman. It's going to be a while before I get to sleep tonight, so I check the news from back home on my phone (which welcomes me back to the Netherlands) when I'm safely tucked into my bed. But perhaps "safely" is the wrong word.

I read of Mia Irazarry, who, wearing a T-shirt with the Puerto Rican flag on it, was preparing a space in a Chicago park she had rented for her twenty-fourth birthday, when sixty-two-year old Timothy Trybus happened by.

"If you're an American citizen," he told her, "you should not be wearing that T-shirt in America."

She tried to explain to the man that Puerto Rico is part of America, but he continued to harangue her. "You are not going to change us," he told her. "You know that. The world is not going to change the United States of America, period."

There it is, the cri de coeur of all nationalists, the idea that nothing should ever change, that change equals corruption, that purity exists and should be preserved.

At the tourist office, I'm met by sixty-six-year old Willem van Gool, a trim, compact man with white hair and an easy smile, who brings me to a room with a map spread on the table of all the enclaves of Baarle-Nassau and Baarle-Hertog. Almost immediately, he starts quizzing me on my knowledge of enclaves. How many enclaves, he asks, are there worldwide? I say I don't know the exact number, but now that the exclaves of India and Bangladesh are no longer in the picture, there are quite a few less.

"Sixty-two," he says, then he asks me how many enclaves the Baarles have. I don't know. "Thirty," he says, "which makes Baarle-

Nassau and Hertog the enclave world champions. By the way, there's no such thing as an exclave. It's not a correct word. It's a wrong word."

I'm not going to argue with him, largely because I don't like to argue and also because I find him charming. If he doesn't want exclaves to exist, then fine, for the duration of my visit to the Baarles they won't exist. His pride of place is uniquely multiple, a love of not one hometown but two, two nationalities, Belgian and Dutch, even his lineage representing this divide that's now cordial but hasn't always been so, his mother Dutch, his father, Belgian. "I was born here and I'm a nationalist," he says with a laugh. "I hate that word."

Willem makes coffees for us both and we sit in front of the enclave map. He shows off a prototype of an enclave passport he's made for people like me who travel around to various enclaves, the front of the "passport" depicting two lions with swords facing one another. He wants to correct the image so that the lions face outwards, the idea being that if you try to do harm to one of the Baarles, you will be "attacked by two pairs of claws."

There are of course problems created by the very nature of two towns in two different countries intersecting one another so intricately. Gray areas in the law sometimes require looking the other way. In the Netherlands, you have to be eighteen to drink, but in Belgium, it's sixteen. So, a lot of Dutch youngsters step into one of the bars in Baarle-Hertog to drink. This practice and some others are greeted with a laissez-faire attitude, the dictum being, Willem says, "Don't be too difficult."

When I first started looking into the Baarles, I had read somewhere of an incident in the 1960s in which a motorcyclist had been thrown from his cycle into a Belgian enclave. The first EMT crew on the scene was Dutch, but they were forbidden from crossing the boundary into Belgium to treat the man. As a consequence, the man died. Before traveling to Baarle, I had looked everywhere for the source of the story, but I couldn't find it. So, I decide to ask Willem if there was any truth to the tale.

As soon as the words, "motorcycle accident," leave my lips, Willem cuts me off.

"You heard that?" he says, putting down his cup.

I don't understand why the question would be so shocking, but I know I have said something wrong.

"That's not true?"

"It gives me a sad feeling," he says softly. "That was my brother."

"What? Oh, I'm so sorry." I never would have brought it up so blithely, or brought it up at all, if I had known that the motorcyclist was Willem's brother. But that kind of coincidence can't be anticipated. I apologize again.

"No, I can live with that," he says. "No problem. It's remarkable that you have heard that."

I mumble something about having been unable to verify it, still mortified for causing Willem obvious pain.

"Okay," he says. "It's correct. It's a very stupid story. It was one of the instigations to make our cooperation better."

His brother and brother's girlfriend had been traveling to a local pub. The owner of the pub was in the car in front, and Willem imagines, though he can't say for certain, that perhaps the two vehicles were playing games. Whatever the case, the motorcycle hit the car and both Willem's brother and the girlfriend were ejected. When a Dutch ambulance crew arrived, they started working with the victims, getting ready to transport them. Everyone knew where the enclaves were but they didn't say anything. But one guy, "perhaps not so clever," suddenly announced, "Hey guys, I think this is Belgium." And that was it. Because this guy had voiced the obvious but unspoken, they couldn't proceed and it took the whole day for a Belgian ambulance crew to arrive. Willem's brother had died instantly when he hit a tree, but the girlfriend was alive when the crew arrived.

Who knows if she would have survived if she had been treated right away? As it was, she lasted only another day.

There were other problems that were not so much the result of the border but as a consequence of the almost inevitable tension of two different groups living side by side. Packs of schoolchildren would cause trouble on their way to school and on their way home, sometimes getting into fights and often trading insults. The Belgian mayor, Alphonse "Fons" Cornelissen, hit on the idea of beginning and ending the school days half an hour apart so that the groups would be less likely to encounter one another in their little packs. The second step in his plan was to initiate a youth camp for the Belgian and Dutch children, the idea being that bringing the children together would also bring the parents along. I just happened to arrive in Baarle-Nassau and Hertog during the week of this annual youth competition: six days of cycling around the countryside, competing in games, and winning trophies, featuring 700 children of mixed Belgian and Dutch teams, and guided by 180 adults, also mixed.

Fons Cornelissen inherited his good sense and creative community spirit from his mother perhaps, a hero of both world wars, Maria Verhoeven. To show me her contributions, Willem drives me several kilometers to the main Belgian-Dutch border, near the village of Zondereignen, distinguished by a towering church spire and surrounded by farm fields. Here in 1915 the Germans constructed a section of electrified border fence in the matter of a day. A group of Dutch children had gone to school in the morning in Belgian Zondereigen and, that afternoon, found themselves trapped by what came to be known as the Deathwire. After negotiations, the children were eventually allowed back, but they couldn't return to school.

The Deathwire killed thousands. This was at a time when virtually no one in the area had electricity and people barely knew what electricity was. At a replicated stretch of the electric fence, photos and text explain some of these casualties, including the gruesome photo of a farmer who had grabbed the fence, obviously thinking it harmless, his body contorted, his hand where he touched the wire, shriveled and blackened. Another plaque tells the story of Louis van den Heuval, who on December 19, 1915, went to the border to deliver a bucket of food to his fifteen-year-old daughter who worked as a maid on the Dutch side. As he tried to deliver the food, a Dutch border guard shot and killed him.

Was he delivering her food for Christmas to remind her of home despite the border separating her from it? I'm reminded of fifteen-year-old Felani Khatun who was shot and killed by the Border Security Forces of India much more recently for the same infraction. I'm reminded of my own fifteen-year-old daughter, safely home in Iowa, who, so far, has never had to approach a border in fear for her life.

Willem, standing next to this now innocuous fence, muses on how people are still being smuggled over borders in the world today, but by different sorts of people and not necessarily for altruistic reasons. I consider how ineffective, yet cruel, walls invariably are. Maria Verhoeven, known locally as Miet Pauw, only a teenager when hostilities began, spent much of the war smuggling people from occupied Belgium to the neutral Netherlands. The replica fence, replete with white porcelain pin insulators spaced regularly like ornaments, has a section that illustrates how people like Verhoeven solved the electric problem. Wearing insulated rubber gloves, they constructed wooden spacers or tunnels, even barrels, for people to crawl through. Searching her house, police found the incriminating gloves and arrested her as a suspected smuggler. But she was released when the war ended not long after. The hated fence was demolished the moment it lost its power, the white porcelain insulators left by the thousands in the fields.

On our way back to Baarle, we pass many groups of children on their bikes competing in this year's sports week, now in its fifty-first year. We stop briefly at the cultural center, situated in an old convent for now, though there are plans to construct a new center with the border running through it. Before Willem drops me off at my hotel, he shows me one other historical curiosity: a tiny enclave of Belgium in town where, during World War I, the Belgians constructed a radio listening and broadcast station. It operated, unmolested by the Germans, because the territory that surrounded it was Dutch, and the Germans in World War I did not want to violate the neutrality of the Netherlands. In World War II, the Germans had no such qualms (as they had invaded the Netherlands *and* Belgium, they were largely uninterested in the technical distinctions between the Baarles).

During this war, Maria Verhoeven once again pitched in, this time helping downed Allied pilots and escaped prisoners find their way to safety. As the First Polish Armored Division was advancing on German lines in 1944, she and two other compatriots were arrested. This time, she was not so fortunate. Less than a month before the Poles liberated the town, she and her fellow resisters were taken away and shot. Today, she's widely remembered and honored by a monument, a street named after her, and photos of her on plaques.

I have never found such self-sacrifice meaningless. On the contrary, the stories of people such as Maria Verhoeven, who sacrifice themselves for strangers, have always moved me tremendously, like the Polish priest, Maximillian Kolbe, who took the place of a stranger at Auschwitz, condemned to death, along with nine others, for the escape of another man from the death camp. I once met a Polish artist in Kraków who chronicles in his photography the repurposing of desecrated Jewish tombstones. He showed me walls that had used tombstones, garden paths, even an entire house made of tombstones. Afterwards, as we sat drinking coffee, he mused aloud, "I ask myself, If I lived during the Second World War, what would I have done? And I don't know. It's an open question. I hope that I would be helping other people, but I'm not that sure of that. I'd like to be sure of that."

In the Baarles, at least, the time is long gone when people died crossing the border to help a loved one, or died defying the border to help a stranger, or because of an absurd technicality that prevented them from being treated for their injuries. Over the years, the border has evolved into a geographical curiosity where the typical tourist picture has you posing with one leg in Belgium and one in the Netherlands.

That evening, I make the mistake once more of reading the news back home, and I learn of a ninety-two-year-old man from Mexico walking in his son's neighborhood in Los Angeles, who was assaulted on July 4 by thirty-year-old Laquisha Jones. Yelling "Go back, go back," she beat him bloody with a brick, enlisting a group of men passing by, telling them falsely he had tried to kidnap her daughter, after which they enthusiastically joined in kicking him while he lay on the ground.

I should probably stop reading the news, but that won't stop these things from happening. Instead, I whistle a little bit of "America" from *West Side Story* and turn out the light by my bed.

The following day, cloudy and slightly chilly, Willem brings me to a vineyard in Baarle-Nassau with a Belgian enclave carved into it. After a few minutes of traipsing through rows of grapes, I spot Belgium thirty meters ahead, marked by a flag poking above the rows. "There it is," I say, perhaps more excited than I should be. "The flag. It's like a game. Find the other country."

We pause at the slightly frayed flag, flapping in the wind as though it senses that it needs to make a proud display. "So now we're in Belgium."

"Now we're in Belgium," he says.

"It looks so different."

"It's warmer now?" he asks.

This tiny parcel of Belgium must have been cultivated in Duke Henry's time, too, as he was mainly interested in land taxes from the cultivated bits. "Do they have to pay Belgian taxes on this part of the vineyard?" I ask.

Willem clears his throat. "Officially, yes, but I do not know."

"There are a lot of gray areas here," I say. "The best thing to do sometimes, I guess, is to just be quiet."

"Yeah," he says, "but the governments do know what is happening, and as long as it is acceptable . . ."

And we leave it at that. *Don't be too difficult.* I decide to change the subject and talk about the grapes. Four types are grown here, I learn, all special hybrids that are bred to be resistant to the cold.

Close Calls with a Potentially
Violent Felon in Cuba

Why had my students and I met in Cuba with a fugitive wanted
by the FBI on thirty-two felony counts, the head of International
Studies wanted to know. Put that way, I suppose it sounded pretty
irresponsible of me, though he hadn't exactly put it that way, because
he didn't know exactly who the American fugitive from justice was.
There were at least seventy living in Cuba. But that's what he meant
when he gave me a call. He also meant: Why are you making my life
and job difficult? I don't recall how he phrased it, but there were
a lot of questions, he said, about my trip, and he sounded nervous
as he recounted the chain of telephone calls that had preceded his
call to me: first, a congressman (he didn't say whom, but most likely
Congressman Mario Díaz-Balart of Florida, whose great aunt was
Fidel Castro's first wife) had called the governor of Iowa, who had
then called the head of the Board of Trustees of the University of
Iowa, who had then called the president of the university, who had
then called the head of International Programs. This was the first
time I recalled ever speaking more than a few words to him, and I
felt a combination of pride that I was the subject of such high-level
scrutiny, panic that I was the subject of such high-level scrutiny,
and the growing certainty that there was now probably an FBI file
with my name on it, a fact that in itself gave me, a highly politicized
child in the 1960s with an older brother and sister who kept me
informed about the protests of the day, a little frisson of pleasure. A

few days earlier, a website called Contacto Latino had reported my trip to Cuba as a symptom of the moral bankruptcy of the Obama administration's "lax" policy in allowing educators such as myself to demean America and its principles by meeting with wanted felons. Three Republican congressmen: Mario Díaz-Balart of Florida, Peter King of New York, and Scott Garrett of New Jersey, had written a letter to President Obama expressing their "outrage that, while on a so-called 'educational' trip to Cuba, permitted by President Obama's weakened sanctions, at least one U.S. university arranged for its students to meet with a potentially violent fugitive from U.S. justice." And José Cárdenas, writing in *Foreign Policy*, said that I had "gushed" about the meeting and speculated that the fugitive we had met with was "likely be either Joanne Chesimard or Charlie Hill, two radicals wanted by U.S. authorities for the murders of U.S. law enforcement officials in the 1970s." Why this was "likely," he never said. We had met neither Charlie Hill nor Chesimard, known more widely as Assata Shakur, the most famous of the American exiles. The article that started all of this and led to the head of International Studies calling me to explain myself was simply an informational piece meant to drum up interest in a short course I was leading with a colleague over the winter break. The reporter had written: "[The professor] said one of the students on the trip last year wrote an excellent piece on an American fugitive who had escaped the country and taken asylum in Cuba. The exile met thirteen UI students who had enrolled in the UI's study abroad program to Cuba last winter." Next thing I knew, I was being accused of endangering students and, worse yet, "gushing."

*

A group of students and faculty from the University of Iowa and Nehanda Abiodun sat in a circle on the balcony of my suite at the Presidente Hotel in the Vedado section of Havana. Nehanda, sunglasses perched on her head, wore orange that day: orange pants, a purple and orange patterned blouse, orange dangling earrings, and an orange tie keeping her roped hair in place. Exuding more of a grandmother aura than that of a bank robber or revolutionary, at sixty-two, Nehanda told us in a soft-spoken voice that she took her name, Nehanda Isoke Abiodun, when she was thirty. The original Nehanda had been a Zimbabwean spiritual leader who led a revolt against the British colonizers and was eventually hanged by them, though reputedly, she wasn't easy to kill. Isoke means a precious gift from God. Abiodun means "born at a time of war." Born in Harlem in 1950, her mother was a "Christian integrationist" and her father was a Muslim nationalist. In 1962, Fidel came to New York and her father took her to see him. At ten, she started her "political career" when she joined a group opposing Columbia's takeover of a gym in the neighborhood. Later graduating from Columbia, she worked at first in a methadone clinic, thinking methadone was a cure for heroin, only to find that methadone "was a worse addiction." She was fired from her job when she refused to administer an increased dosage to one of the patients. At the time, heroin addiction was devastating the black community and a group of activists, including members of the Black Panthers, the Young Lords, Republic of New Africa, and SDS, simply took over a part of Lincoln Hospital by occupying it, a move that was at first met by the police surrounding the hospital, but eventual acquiescence and a rather remarkable turnaround. The hospital administration reluctantly agreed to the program and the Lincoln Detox Center was born. Nehanda claims a success rate of 75 to 80 percent because "the people who were addicted were no longer parasites but contributors to the community." It ran until 1979, when Mayor Ed Koch "sent a SWAT team to close the clinic, because it was a training center 'for terrorists.'"

This is how she tells it, and of course in such hotly contested histories, who's telling the story makes all the difference. The first time we met her, American journalist Tom Miller, who has known Nehanda for many years, warned in advance that she didn't want to discuss the charges against her, which include bank robbery, escape from prison, and racketeering, and that first time she didn't. She talked almost exclusively about what it was like to live in exile. Understandably, or at least predictably, her views on the charges against her favored a narrative of struggle against oppression. Accused of helping free convicted bank robber and cop killer Assata Shakur from prison in 1979, she used the word "liberated" and wanted us to understand the difference between that word and "escaped," which all of us understood, but whether we sympathized with her version was another matter. Among our group on my first visit was a student who had interned the previous summer for a conservative anti-Castro think tank. Our guide, Lian, took me aside one day and asked what I knew of him, what his story was. Obviously, the Castro government was watching. Lian, with whom we all got along fabulously, was nonetheless the daughter of a well-known Cuban journalist and, like all guides, vetted for loyalty. She wanted to know, though not in so many words, whether he was a spy. On another occasion at the National Art Museum, I wanted to show my students some paintings displayed in a corner of the museum that were implicitly critical of Castro. Lian scolded me. "Remember where you are," she said, indicating the cameras watching us and two elderly women near us, perhaps listening. Later, she told me I had made the mistake of calling him "Castro," which was how his enemies referred to him, while his supporters called him "Fidel." On this second visit, one of our students was a young woman whose grandparents and mother had fled the Castro regime and whose family, like so many others, had lost practically everything they owned when they left. Her mother and sister joined her on the trip, and my colleague and I allowed her to split off a few times from the rest of the group to explore with her family all that they had lost in the revolution. The sisters had never visited Cuba before, and her mother had left as a young child in 1960, but she had raised them to speak Spanish and carry proudly the legacy of their family's roots.

Nehanda didn't tell us how she managed to escape to Cuba in the early 1990s, only that she had to do so. "I'll be real honest with you," she told us. "I didn't want to come to Cuba, because I thought I had a responsibility to my community. But there came a time when it became clear to everybody but me that I was going to be captured. I saw it coming—I wasn't even in the U.S. when I came. The thing that convinced me—the people who loved me said if you're captured it's a victory for our enemies. If you come to Cuba, it's a victory for us. If I'm in prison, there's very little I can do." A case in point, she mentioned only in passing: Geronimo Pratt, a high-ranking official of the Black Panthers whom the FBI wanted removed, and through its counterintelligence program framed Pratt for a murder he couldn't have committed, because he was 350 miles away at the time of the murder. He became a suspect only when a paid FBI informant accused him. After spending twenty-seven years in prison, the first eight years in solitary confinement, the charges against him were vacated and he was awarded $4.5 million for false imprisonment. He died a few years later, spending his money to try to free other victims of "Cointelpro" languishing in prison.

She put her head on the table when asked what she'd done to build freedom in Cuba. She's known here as the "Godmother of Cuban Hip-Hop," a title that she's proud of, as well as being Tupac Shakur's godmother (Tupac was Assata Shakur's nephew by marriage). "And I don't even like hip-hop," she said, the class laughing in response. Now she mentored medical students from the U.S. whom, she admitted proudly, "lifted my breasts for me." She prepared them home-cooked meals and talked to them about what they were going to do with their medical degrees in the U.S. She talked about social responsibility. "If you're willing to listen to me, you can be one of my babies. I like argument. You do not have to agree with me. The biggest problem is lack of history, misinformation." At this point, our Cuban-American student told Nehanda about her own family story, about her grandfather refusing to work as a doctor for Fidel, their house being vandalized, and having to leave the country as a result. Nehanda listened sympathetically, admitting there were mistakes that were made and that she wasn't going to tell this young woman not to feel the way she did, but she just wanted her to come to Cuba and make up her own mind. That's exactly what we had done. When the head of International Studies called me and asked what I was doing meeting with a felon, I pointed out that the U.S. doesn't require journalists to hold the same political views as the subjects of their interviews. That seemed more like something an oppressive country such as, say, Cuba, might make as a prerequisite. He took my point, but he had wanted to know if I was planning to meet with the fugitive again.

"Planning?" I asked. "No, I'm not planning on meeting her, but if the opportunity arises . . ."

"Fair enough," he said, "Of course, I'm not forbidding you, but you won't go out of your way . . ."

It seemed to me he was forbidding me without actually forbidding me, but we both pretended he wasn't. Congressman Díaz-Balart and his fellow signers of the letter to Obama complained that we had dared to expose such impressionable young minds to a potentially violent felon, and how disrespectful that was toward the police officers who had been killed by Nehanda's confederates. Respect or disrespect had nothing to do with it. We weren't indoctrinating them. We were simply exposing them to different points of view. My colleague and I were leading a writing course. And so, despite the disapproval of some of my country's politicians and the tacit disapproval of my own Study Abroad office, we exposed our students a second time to a "potentially violent felon" on the rooftop of the

Presidente Hotel with a view of the sea and the famous promenade known as the Malecón.

I suppose she might have, on a whim, pulled out a pair of six-guns in the spirit of Yosemite Sam, aimed them at our feet, and yelled, "Dance, Varmints," before blasting away. But remarkably, she didn't. Instead, we were privy to an extraordinary scene: Nehanda and our Cuban-American student hugging and the young woman saying, "I love you," which at that moment seemed possible. Not "I agree with you" or "I admire all your choices." But a simple and heartfelt moment, one of the most important moments for this young woman of the entire trip, when she was given permission from a fugitive from U.S. justice to feel however she was going to feel. And the moment, you could see, was important for this old revolutionary as well, whose mother had died three years earlier and who hadn't seen her for thirty years before that.

"I'm going to tell you a story," she said. "I'm sitting on the sidewalk waiting by the Capitolio. Going through a litany of things that are wrong with my life, and I see this young couple with this little baby that's maybe one years old who's just learning to walk and his father has one hand. The mother has the other hand. There comes a moment when he says leave me alone," and she pantomimed the baby looking up at his parents. "I can see in his face, I've got my mom and my pop to hold me up. I've got this." She took three baby steps. "I've got people who will lift me up if I fall. That baby saved my life at that moment. So you ask me how I survive. I sometimes forget I've got people who hold me up. Talking to you saves my life. It gives me purpose. That's how I see it."

As I saw it, the potential of violence in meeting Nehanda was that of cognitive dissonance. That there were many things wrong with the way the Black Panthers and their associates had worked for social justice seemed obvious, certainly in the banks that were robbed, the guards and policemen murdered. But the government's way of handling its opponents was often just as criminal—how many Geronimo Pratts were railroaded or gunned down by racist police and FBI agents? Many mistakes had been made, and some things had been right about both sides. Moral myopia might be satisfying, but rarely is it smart. While it's so much easier to punish a person than a state—after all, we know how many counts there are against Nehanda—neither the U.S. nor Cuba had clean hands. Both countries committed crimes against their own dissenting citizens in the name of officially lofty ideals. Our crime against America was in meeting Nehanda with our students and listening to her story. Our crime was that we chose in a small way to press the reset button and move, if only in baby steps, toward reconciliation.

5. Courtesy of the author.

They Have Forgotten Many Things

> The essence of a nation is that all individuals
> have many things in common; and also that
> they have forgotten many things.
>
> ERNEST RENAN

My new Argentinian friend Ezequiel and I sit near the pool table, sipping our local Longdon Pride beers when he spots the most famous guy in the Falklands. On the day of the referendum last March, this guy danced to the polls covered head to toe in a suit and shoes bedecked with Union Jacks. The Victory Bar, packed with Falkland Islanders on this Friday night, is a British pub to outdo all British pubs, with bunting everywhere as well as a picture of two bulldogs with the caption, "What we've got, we'll Hold." This is one of the most isolated communities in the world, both politically and geographically, but you wouldn't know it by the way they make a crowd in their isolation, reminding me of the hundreds of huddled penguins I saw this afternoon at their remote rookeries on the island, almost otherworldly in the way they seem oblivious to anyone else.

As far as foregone conclusions go, not even North Korea could have staged less of a nail-biter than this referendum on whether to remain a British Overseas Territory or not. What you must understand is that there are fewer than three thousand people in the Falklands, a group of islands off the southeast tip of South America, about the size of Connecticut. Settlers have come from the British

Isles since 1833, and most Falkland Islanders can trace their English roots back generations. It is more of a village state than a city-state, and for as long as anyone can remember, they have told the world ad nauseam that they are British through and through, though England has at times rejected them, Argentina has despised them, and the rest of the world has largely ignored them. Of the 1,516 votes cast in the referendum, 1,513 voters cast yes votes and three people voted no. That perhaps was the only surprise: that there were as many as three Falkland Islanders who didn't want to be British. The president of Argentina, Cristina Kirchner, likewise had a predictable reaction. She called the vote, "a referendum of squatters." Most of the Islanders I've met think of her as a "nutter," but her recent saber-rattling has made them nervous, living as they do in Argentina's shadow. The "victory" alluded to in the bar's name is the victory of England over Argentina in the seventy-four-day Falklands War in 1982, preceded by Argentina's invasion of the islands. No mere referendum could change this uncomfortable status quo, in place since the end of the war when the territory became a military fortress, the airport itself a British base. Possession of the Falklands, known as the Malvinas to the Argentines, is enshrined in Argentina's constitution.

The Union Jack man is wearing an Adidas shirt now, but Ezequiel still wants his photo taken with him. Clearly drunk, the man obliges and seems intrigued by Ezequiel's interest, as an Argentine, in the Falklands. In that way that all travelers are transformed into symbols of their nations, Ezequiel might as well be dressed head to toe in Argentine flags as far as this man is concerned. This is not a good look in the Victory Bar.

"What's your opinion on the Falklands?" he asks Ezequiel. "Have you had any of your impressions changed?"

Ezequiel starts to speak, but the man barrels on. "If Argentina just accepted the Falkland Islanders, everyone could get along just fine. Am I right?"

"You're probably right," Ezequiel, who is small and thin and looking rather vulnerable, says with an uncomfortable smile.

Meanwhile, a man who is three Union Jacks to the wind, dressed in coat and tie, gravitates toward me. I have a bad feeling about him. He seems curious about Ezequiel, so I introduce myself as an American.

"Oh, I thought you were an Argie," he says. "Then I'd have to knock your head in."

"I'm American," I repeat.

"You work for a news service?" Another trick question. The only people that make Falkland Islanders more suspicious than Argentines are journalists. Earlier in the week, a largely toothless woman in her seventies approached me and, by way of introduction, said, "You're not paparazzi, are you? Asking a lot of silly questions and taking a lot of photographs where you're not supposed to."

"No," I said.

"Good. Then I'll talk to you." I didn't especially want to talk to her, but she seemed convinced that, as a Falkland Islander, she had things to say that needed saying. She proceeded to chat about how windy it was, the blizzard of '75, her dog's monthly cycle, and how she hates forest fires. It didn't seem to matter to her that it's *always* windy here and that the Falklands are treeless. "You can replace trees," she told me, "but not the little animals."

"I'm a professor," I tell the young man who wants to knock in the head of an Argie or a journalist. "Are you a Falkland Islander?"

He nods, sways, touches his tie.

I ask him what his profession is.

"I'm in the military," he says. "I was just at a mate's funeral."

I offer my condolences, which he ignores as he proceeds to bang on about how Britain gave Argentina democracy. "If not for '82," he says, "they wouldn't have democracy. We gave it to them. Few people realize that." Perhaps I don't look suitably impressed because

I'm trying to work that out in my head. Yes, a despicable military junta, wanting to take pressure off the faltering Argentine economy and the crimes against thousands of its own citizens it had "disappeared," embarked on a jingoistic military adventure to invade the Malvinas, retake what Argentina sees as rightfully theirs, and thus restore the government's legitimacy—which seemed to work until the British, under Prime Minister Margaret Thatcher, sent an expeditionary force and recaptured the islands. Not long after that the junta collapsed. But to see this as the Falkland Islanders *giving* democracy to the Argentinians seemed a stretch. There didn't seem to be much altruism in either direction.

Apparently, this man doesn't much care for Americans, either, and he says something slurred that I can't make out except for "CIA."

"Your people put them in power in the first place, fucked everything up."

My people? Now, here I am, clearly dressed head to toe in Old Glory, at least in his eyes. I don't know what to say to him. I antagonize him simply by existing.

"I live in Singapore," I say. It's not much. But it's all I've got left to avoid a head knocking.

"You a Yank?" he says.

"Yes, I'm American."

"I'm a Brit," he says. "No matter where I am in the world, I'll always be British."

I think it's best at this point to try to get Ezequiel and myself away from this guy as soon as possible. I give Ezequiel a nod and he says goodbye to the famous Falklander. As we leave, my belligerent friend, bedecked with Union Jacks invisible to the naked eye, approaches the other guy and starts asking him about Ezequiel. But we leave before the man gains any valuable intelligence. Under the circumstances, it feels like an escape. Truly, while I'm an outsider in many places in the world, I've never felt more displaced than in the Falklands.

*

Safely back at my B&B that evening, I wonder what exactly the drunk soldier meant by "British." I doubt he knows, but I, though American, have given it some thought, and Ezequiel, though Argentine, has probably given Britishness more thought than anyone else in the Falklands. Ezequiel and I met by chance during the week, he researching his PhD dissertation titled "Empire Redux: The Falklands and the End of Greater Britain," me on a fool's errand.

I'm visiting these fabled and controversial Brits of the South Atlantic, often described as "more British than the British," to see how they celebrate Guy Fawkes Day, that most British of holidays. To my American mind, raised on Fourth of July spectacles of patriotism and fireworks, Guy Fawkes is an odd national holiday, celebrating not a declaration of independence (from whom might the Brits declare independence but themselves?), but a failed attempt to burn down Parliament by a Frenchman whose mustachioed visage has been adopted by those most mischievous of anarchists, "Anonymous."

Unfortunately, upon my arrival in the Falkland's capital of Stanley, I learned that Guy Fawkes is perhaps the only vestige of Britishness that no one in the Falklands cares a fig about. Anything else with a shred of Britishness is clung to like a life vest in stormy seas—from the cottage pie my landlady fixes for supper, to the six o'clock news from London, which is on a three-hour delay so that it comes on at six in the Falklands, nearly eight thousand miles away, to those red phone booths, virtually extinct in England, but brought to Stanley in 1988 and standing sentinel ever since on its streets. Until fairly recently, a London cab was the official car of the governor. So it wasn't completely daft of me to expect joyous Islanders lighting bonfires and shooting fireworks into the sky of the Southern Hemisphere to further convince anyone who'll listen that they're loyal Brits.

Fireworks ended Guy Fawkes in the Falklands. The British military in recent years has forbidden the shipment of fireworks into the Falklands on Ministry of Defense flights, and fireworks scare the old people, reminding them of that awful night in '82 when an errant British shell landed on a house and killed three women seeking shelter there. Guy Fawkes has lost its relevance, but not Halloween, which was widely celebrated in American fashion a week earlier.

*

Nearly a hundred years to the day before the outbreak of the Falklands War, Ernest Renan wrote that a nation's "unity is always effected through brutality" and that "the essence of a nation is that all individuals have many things in common; and also that they have forgotten many things."

Since 1982, the Falkland Islanders have been in the process of forgetting the cultural mélange that formed them. "Camp," a hybrid culture born of Britain and Patagonia, the word derives from the Spanish "campo" for countryside, redolent with the history of Patagonia. In the minds of Falkland Islanders, Camp looms large, separated by a cultural chasm from Stanley. Camp used to be even more distinct from Stanley, with its own time zone, one hour behind this small town of Land Rovers and brightly colored tin and steel roofs. When the countryside dominated their lives, there was an interdependence and tolerance. "People who arrive now feel that they've come to another suburb," says John Fowler, an émigré from England who's lived in the Falklands since 1971 and was once editor of the local paper, the *Penguin News*. "Because of the threat from Argentina, we have tended to reject those aspects of our history that have less to do with being British."

Before they were enemies, Falkland Islanders and Argentines shared a common history, particularly in Patagonia. Before the war, the Falklands were simply known as "the islands" in Patagonia without any clarification needed. And in the Falklands, Patagonia was referred to as "the coast" or "the mainland" without differentiating between parts that belonged to Chile or Argentina. Until the 1880s, the only European settlements of any size south of Buenos Aires were Carmen de Patagones in the north, Punta Arenas in the south, the Falklands to the east, and a colony in the middle settled by hundreds of Welsh eager to escape Britishness and to preserve their own language and traditions. Sheep were the links between these settlements. Between 1885 and 1886, forty thousand sheep were transported between the Falklands and Santa Cruz Province in Argentina. The route between these lands could be traced, the story goes, by the sheep carcasses floating in the sea.

The people of the Falklands and Patagonia crisscrossed these territories, too, the gaucho culture of Patagonia present in the islands and the Islanders settling quite regularly on the mainland. The populations were small, only a couple of thousand in either place, but 10 percent of the Falkland Island population moved in the 1880s to Patagonia. Many of the farms they founded in Patagonia in the nineteenth century are still owned by their descendants and Falkland Island surnames still exist in Patagonia. The regional roots of these families go deeper than those of most current Patagonians. The Falkland Islanders and the Argentines of today might choose to forget these links or simply ignore them in favor of the murkiness of territorial claims.

In his "Conquest of the Desert," General Julio Argentino Roca led a campaign in the 1870s against the indigenous peoples of Patagonia with a six thousand man army, killing fifteen hundred, capturing fifteen thousand, and forcing them off their lands, forcing them into servitude, and preventing them from reproducing. Roca, formerly a hero, more recently branded a genocidal murderer, had his name removed from streets and public buildings under Cristina Kirchner's reign, his likeness removed from the hundred-peso bill and replaced with Evita Perón's.

What neither the Falkland Islanders or the Argentines will ever forget is a murky and endlessly debatable episode from 1833 when the islands were merely the islands, the coast was merely the coast, and all claims were contingent. To an outsider like myself, it's all rather tedious in the way that children's arguments about who hit whom first are tedious. But it's clearly all the fault of an equally murky character named Louis Vernet, a merchant from Buenos Aires, a Huguenot originally from Hamburg, who was more of an opportunist than a representative of anyone's interest but his own, seeking approval from both the British and Buenos Aires for a colony at Port Louis in the Falklands. Whether he and his business partners had any standing to represent Argentina officially is up for grabs. Vernet seemed to think he had the authority to capture three American fishing vessels for illegally sealing, though the Americans disagreed and sent the naval ship, *Lexington*, to raid the place. The Americans spiked Vernet's guns, arresting him and six other senior members of the colony for piracy, led them away in chains, and took the rest of the settlement except for some gauchos on board. Mostly Germans from Buenos Aires, the would-be colonists, who seemed thrilled by their capture, wrote Captain Silas Duncan and "appeared greatly rejoiced at the opportunity thus presented of removing with their families from a desolate region where the climate is always cold and cheerless and the soil extremely unproductive."

Buenos Aires complained to the Americans that Vernet was their governor and that he had the right to seize ships. The Americans eventually let the lot go after which the Argentines sent a garrison to the islands. The soldiers hated the place, too, quickly mutinied, and murdered their commanding officer. Shortly after the mutiny was put down, the British arrived, expelled the garrison, and found a group of unhappy gauchos who complained that Vernet was paying them in worthless paper, redeemable only at his stores, and they were deeply in debt to him.

The colony was reestablished only to have disaster strike again, when the gauchos, aided by some escaped convicts, murdered Matthew Brisbane, an associate of Vernet's, and other senior members of the colony. When twenty-four-year-old Charles Darwin sailed into Port on the *Beagle* some months later, he had this assessment:

"After the possession of these miserable islands had been contested by France, Spain, and England, they were left uninhabited. The government of Buenos Aires then sold them to a private individual, but likewise used them, as old Spain had done before, for a penal settlement. England claimed her right and seized them. The Englishman who was left in charge of the flag was consequently murdered. A British officer was next sent, unsupported by any power: and when we arrived, we found him in charge of a population, of which rather more than half were runaway rebels and murderers."

Now these "miserable islands" claim Darwin, too: a small settlement named for him, despite his disdain, where he reputedly spent a night, which later became the haunt of gauchos and saw heavy fighting during the Falklands War. Argentine soldiers who gave up their lives for their nation's version of the events of 1833 now permanently reside here under rows of white crosses.

*

"I often tell myself," Renan wrote, "that an individual who had those faults which in nations are taken for good qualities, who fed off vainglory, who was to that degree jealous, egotistical, and quarrelsome, and who would draw his sword on the smallest pretext, would be the most intolerable of men."

If countries were people, most of us would pretend not to be home when they came calling. Some would register somewhere on the scale as psychopathic. While the famous Argentine author Jorge Luis Borges likened Argentina and the UK to two bald men fighting over a comb, I would clarify that by the outbreak of the hostilities between the two old men, they'd been fighting for that comb, off and on, since they'd had full heads of hair.

In 1933, the UK issued a stamp commemorating the Falkland Islands' centenary as a British colony. When mail with the stamp affixed arrived in Argentina, it was treated the same as a letter arriving without any stamp at all: postage due, the stamp itself obliterated with cancellation markings. In 1936, Argentina retaliated with a Malvinas stamp of its own. Given the ability of the smallest symbols to stir nationalistic pride, these postage stamp wars might have erupted into full-scale conflict, given the right conditions. The UK and the United States nearly went to war once over an American pig that was shot by a British subject in the once-disputed San Juan Islands for crossing a border and eating the Irishman's vegetables.

But it wasn't until the 1960s that the Falklands conflict truly heated up, with Argentina bringing the issue to the United Nations. Not that the Brits were all that eager anymore to hold onto their colonies. After the devastation and expense of World War II, it was fire sale time for the British Empire whose slogan might as well have been "What We've Got, We'll Hold . . . for a Modest Down Payment." One of the principles applied to this downsizing was the right of self-determination. White Brits, and this was largely the demographic of the time, were just out of luck when it came to Rhodesia and self-determination. They were a decided minority within a largely black country, and the English were more embarrassed than proud of the overseas colonials. The British government was just as eager to divorce itself from Argentines of British descent. As one British diplomat wrote of the Anglo-Argentines, their society "has for many years been a grotesque parody of English life as it might have been in the 20's. We should not mourn its passing." The colonies, for England, were no longer a source of pride as they had been in 1898 when an overzealous postmaster general in Canada issued a stamp with the slogan, "We hold a Vaster Empire than has Been," showing the Falklands among the possessions, but also a few territories that had never been British, including Borneo, parts of German Africa, Portuguese Africa, and assorted bits of other countries.

The loyal Falkland Islanders presented a unique problem for England in that the Kelpers, as they called themselves, had replaced no indigenous population, so the matter of self-determination was not as clear-cut a moral decision as in Rhodesia or other colonies. The Kelpers resisted every attempt to brush them aside. In promoting their Britishness to the Brits, the Falkland Islanders from the late 1940s onwards touted their "100 percent" whiteness, culminating in a 1979 incident when the islands refused to accept a group of Vietnamese refugees to their community, so as not to dilute their perceived Britishness. To its credit, the *Penguin News* wrote an editorial denouncing this move: "By maintaining our population of British origin we are making a grave mistake and are developing a sense of bigoted racial superiority in our people. We have much to gain and (as long as racism is excluded) nothing to lose from admitting settlers of *any* race. We desperately need people."

In order to convince the stubborn population that, sooner or later, the Argentine flag would fly above the islands, the British government, from the sixties onwards, sent a series of representatives to the Falklands. Three possible solutions were explored: condominium, in which Argentina and the UK would exercise joint sovereignty over the islands (an idea that both Argentina and the Kelpers rejected outright); leaseback (in which the Kelpers would lease the islands from Argentina for a set number of years, much as in the case of

Hong Kong); or "euthanasia by generous compensation," in which the Kelpers would be bribed away from the islands.

When Nicholas Ridley, minister of state at the Foreign and Commonwealth Office, arrived in the Falklands in November of 1980, he tried to sell the Kelpers on leaseback, and if gentle persuasion wouldn't work, then he didn't mind threatening them. If the Falkland Islanders didn't come to some accommodation, then they would have to "take the consequences," he told them. This statement, among many other veiled threats, infuriated them, and they saw him off with boos and placards, Union Jacks waving, and car horns blaring. Ridley was not the only government official exasperated by the Falkland Islanders. The British ambassador to Colombia wrote, "Surely the time has come for HMG [Her Majesty's Government] to let the inhabitants of the Islands know that they are a nuisance and make it clear that if they want a better life they ought to seek it elsewhere rather than look to HMG to make the Islands pleasanter for them." To make matters worse, Ridley had struck a secret deal with Argentina in New York *before* consulting with the Islanders, and their noisy sendoff of Ridley was nothing compared to the reception he received when he returned to London. The Islanders had their supporters in the Parliament. In December of 1980, Ridley was laid into by eighteen MPs who thought it shameful that HMG would want to abandon a people who were "wholly British in blood and sentiment." Back in the Falklands, one of the Island's councillors argued in a New Year's message that leaseback "might suit the people of Hong Kong—they were never consulted in the first place, and they are Chinese anyway." But not the Kelpers.

Yes, those pesky Hong Kong Chinese were certainly making it difficult for "abandoned Brits" the world over. In 1981, the British Nationality Act was passed, stipulating that anyone claiming British identity had to have a parent who was a British citizen, and because Britishness was understood largely at that time to be something restricted to white people, the "kith and kin" of the Anglo-Saxons, they didn't see the Hong Kong Chinese as citizens, and they didn't want them. About a third of the population of the Falklands didn't qualify as Brits under this act either, and they joined the thousands of abandoned Brits the world over, from white Rhodesians, to the residents of Belize, formerly British Honduras, who could claim nothing but heritage after 1981.

Given the mixed signals the British were putting out, it's no wonder the Argentines had no idea how the Brits felt about the Malvinas. They knew that the British wanted to be rid of the Falkland Islands, but it was taking an awfully long time. And the junta, murdering its young people and presiding over a tanking economy, desperately needed a strong shot of nationalism to bolster support. Maybe all Britain needed was a little nudge.

The final signal to both Islanders and Argentina that the Kelpers were on their own came in June of 1981 when the Thatcher government announced that it would withdraw the ice patrol boat, HMS *Endurance*, from the South Atlantic, leaving the Falklands more vulnerable than ever.

Less than a year later, on April 2, 1982, Argentine forces invaded the Falkland Islands.

It's one thing to give away your useless comb to the bald man across the ocean, but when he takes it by force . . . ? Suddenly, there was no more sacred piece of British soil than the peat and rock of the Falklands. "We are all Falklanders now," the *London Times* proclaimed with that sentimental trope that has attended so many international crises since the blockade of West Berlin by the Soviets when John Kennedy rousingly told the world he was a Berliner (and it's not exactly true that he mistakenly proclaimed himself a jelly donut, a "Berliner," as popular lore goes). The *Times* had it turned around in any event—the Falklanders wanted to be Brits. They didn't want the Brits to become Falklanders.

How the Thatcher government reacted and why has been the subject of much speculation over the years. Within a day, Margaret Thatcher had secured the support she needed to send an expeditionary force sailing across the Atlantic to hold on to a small colony that most Brits had no notion even existed. Some in England confused the Falklands with the Shetlands and wondered what the Argentines were doing invading England. Perhaps the Islanders should just hop over to Scotland until hostilities ended. Some in Parliament voiced their dismay as well. One Labour minister lamented, "We went to bed on Thursday in 1982 and woke up on Friday in 1882." In the *Guardian*, Peter Jenkins expressed his surprise logically, if a bit haughtily: "The Islanders cannot wish the British Empire back into existence . . . they cannot determine that the whole of British foreign policy be directed toward the creation of a world safe for South Atlantic sheep shearers."

But that's exactly what happened. The Falklands were recaptured after seventy-four days and the Falkland Islanders were given everything they had always wanted and more: an exclusive two hundred mile fishing zone, a new airport, near complete self-governance except for defense, and above all, British citizenship.

All was forgiven. All was forgotten.

On my visit years later, a gray-haired man with wire rims stood at a public meeting with candidates for a local election, in the same hall where Nicholas Ridley was booed by residents for trying to sell them on leaseback, and asked the candidates not the toughest question of the night, but the one that carried the most weight, the most emotion. He wanted to know what metal the proposed bust of Maggie Thatcher, who had died seven months prior to this meeting, would be cast in. "Mother Falklands," he intoned, "our savior, the Baroness, deserves the best." He insisted that the material should be bronze, that it should last for centuries. "I think we should do the best for the lady," he pled before he sat down. No one among the twelve candidates disagreed. It wasn't even an issue and, besides, if anyone dared say otherwise, he or she would risk receiving a total of three votes, those three mysterious and unpatriotic naysayers who don't want the Falklands to be British anymore.

If Maggie Thatcher is in heaven, it must look a lot like the Falklands.

*

Thirty plus years after the war, the world is indeed safe for South Atlantic sheep shearers and their sheep, though not so much for their cows. Adrian Lowe has lost half a dozen cows to land mines over the years on his beach, but no sheep. "You have to be a hundred pounds to set them off," he says. "Sheep are all right. Cows don't stand a chance." Minefield signs with skulls and crossbones are as common here as animal crossing signs elsewhere in the world, the skull and crossbones mouse pads sold along with Falkland Island hats made in China in the local gift shops. Fourteen years ago, Adrian and his wife, Lisa, started diversifying by taking day-trippers from the cruise liners on their brief stopover to Antarctica to the penguin rookery on their property, Rock Office, where thousands of penguins nest along a craggy shoreline, or Falkland War veterans to memorials and graveyards to pay respects to their fallen comrades.

"A really good gather," Adrian says, pointing to the crest of the hill at a mob of sheep his wife, Lisa, and son have herded to be sheared this Saturday. He walks with a bit of a limp as he steps from his aged Land Rover to close a gate behind us on the farm he and Lisa run with their children, ten thousand acres, only of moderate size in the Falklands. Adrian, in his fifties, originally from England, has lived in the Falklands for forty-four years, but he's a relative newcomer. Lisa's family has lived here for five generations.

A hundred years ago, Adrian would have been the typical Falkland Islander: a shearer of almost unparalleled skill, though a hundred years ago he wouldn't have owned his farm but would have worked for the omnipresent Falkland Island Company.

"I'm only five miles out of town," Adrian tells me as we take an off-road circuit of East Falkland in his Rover, but I'm Camp, definitely Camp." Adrian frets that everyone wants to live in Stanley and the traditions of Camp are being forgotten, children growing up in Stanley, not even taught their own history by the imported teachers from Australia and the UK. Not even the '82 conflict.

Journalists in '82 called the landscape "barren and windswept," which likewise annoys Adrian. "It was winter anyway." Regardless of the season, an outsider's first impression as he or she travels the forty minutes by car over a gravel road from the airport into Stanley will almost certainly be that of a melancholy landscape, wind-stripped hills, and rivers of rock people call "stone runs." Adrian sees something different. The land is windswept, but it's also one of the most beautiful spots in the world, his home worth defending.

As we bump mile over bumpy mile, past stagnant ponds, white grass, and diddle dee, a heather-like bush reminiscent of Scotland, an upland goose trots along, taking off like a cargo plane fully loaded; seven ewes and two lambs run in front of the Rover; a fjord, like something in Iceland, commands a view of rugged hills and sea; and several seemingly unperturbed cows seem stranded on an island the size of a football field. Adrian points out the places where the wind has eroded the grasses, the best places to dig peat, he says. If it's too fluffy it goes straight up the chimney, and you have to cut it so that the hole doesn't make a hazard for cows and cyclists. There's enough peat for Adrian to heat his home and cook with for the next million years, he says. And it's free.

As he's talking, the road goes white with hail, over which nothing can be heard. The hail, after some minutes of our waiting in the heated cab, decreases but turns into a heavy snow squall, none of which deters Adrian, who says that in the days when sheep herding was done on horseback, if you hit a storm like this, you'd put on your waterproofs, turn your sheepskin over your horse, and seek shelter by a rock or in front of the horse. Stepping out of the Rover, he opens another gate, more bothered by his bad hip than the torrent of sleet and hailstones. On any given day, snow is possible—too bad those old journalists who misjudged the Falklands, according to Adrian, didn't visit in summer like me.

At Goose Green, the scene of some of the heaviest fighting of the war, we stop at the Galley Café, a former mess hall for farm workers that used to feed a hundred workers at a time. The café, mostly empty except for one other couple, is decorated with de rigueur Union Jacks on its ceiling, blue plastic chairs and checkered tablecloths, military memorabilia on the walls, photos of the war, illustrations of military equipment, a map of the Falklands, and an old-fashioned wall phone. Looking out the window, you might expect to see Charles Darwin collecting fossils along the beach, or the schoolhouse on fire as paratroopers close in. The one big change that Adrian noticed when we first pulled in was the absence of the letters POW on the shearing shed. This is where captured Argentines were held at first, and where the letters remained for thirty years.

"What a shame it is that POW has come off the shearing shed," Adrian tells the other two customers. "Someone was naughty."

"It's about time," the woman says.

But Adrian disagrees. "It's a part of history," he says.

*

By the outbreak of the war, one hundred thousand or so Anglo-Argentines lived in Argentina, the largest population of Anglo descendants outside of Britain and North America. Jorge Luis Borges had a grandmother who was English. The Anglos of Buenos Aires sent their children to British schools, spoke English at home, joined the British Club, and shopped at Harrods, the only branch of the famed London department store outside of England.

When war broke out, the Anglos felt as though the two halves of their identity were at war with one another, the vast majority supporting Argentina's claims on the Malvinas, but viewing themselves as fervent supporters of the Queen as well. They sent letters to newspapers in England and Argentina, to MPs, and to the Queen herself, begging the English to reconsider their expeditionary force. The response from the Thatcher government was cool—at best, some sympathized with their plight, but no one was going to call back the warships to ease their psychic pain.

In Argentina, symbols of Britishness were quickly banished or modified. A portrait of Queen Elizabeth was removed from the British Club in Rio Gallegos and the front plate was replaced with the words "British Club," but in Spanish. They couldn't be loyal to both countries, or to both ideas of themselves, though they tried.

Early in the conflict, before British ships reached the Falklands, a delegation of Anglo-Argentines visited the islands to reassure the Islanders that life under Argentinian rule would not be much different for them, but the Kelpers would have none of it. To the Kelpers, the Anglo-Argentines were Argentines, or at best imitation Brits, not real Brits like them (though a third of the Kelpers no longer qualified as Brits either under the British Nationality Act). The Argentines offered at least to take care of the children of the Falkland Islanders in Buenos Aires, where they would be safe for the war's duration, but the Kelpers refused the offer.

The result of these dual snubs from the Thatcher government and the Falkland Islanders was a tectonic shift in the identities of most Anglo-Argentines. They felt betrayed, abandoned, and no longer what they thought they had always been. One woman wrote to an Argentine newspaper: "I used to visit Great Britain and every time I arrived there I felt like I was at home. From now on, I will never set foot on British soil." Another turned in her British passport. A third slammed the Falkland Islanders as "idiots" for not accepting their offer of safe haven for their children.

The war taught the Anglo-Argentines not to fetishize a Britain that proved to be a well-loved mirage that could easily evaporate within the span of seventy-four days. From now on, they were Argentines. By 1998, Harrods had shut its doors, the English Social Club in Lomas de Zamora struggled to retain members, and the venerable Richmond Tea Rooms were transformed into a Nike outlet.

*

Falkland Islanders are sensitive. It's unimaginable that Argentina will invade again, but Cristina Kirchner makes trouble on the international stage, lining up allies against them. When Ezequiel Mercau, the Argentine graduate student writing about Britishness, arrived on the island, he was interviewed by the local radio station, but he had to do three takes because he kept inadvertently using words that the interviewer, a Falkland Islander, felt might be misinterpreted. When he said that he hoped there would come a time when there was more open dialogue between the Islanders and Argentina, he was told that some Islanders would react strongly to that, the idea of talking to Argentina repugnant to them. When Ezequiel called the Falkland Islanders "residents" of the islands, he made another misstep. "Residents" sounds temporary.

If nations sprung up like volcanoes, then the Falklands would still be spewing lava, though slowed to a trickling river. The Falkland Islands, though ancient, might as well have formed in 1982, when their world changed, *forever*, I'm tempted to say. Although nations try to pretend otherwise, there's no such thing as forever.

Despite referenda to the contrary and their incessant loyalty to a long-gone British Empire, the islands seem to be coalescing into a new sense of nationhood. The majority of Falkland Islanders, according to a 2012 census, see themselves as Falkland Islanders first, Brits second, though the crack of daylight between the two is only a sliver.

As early as 1984, there were those who suggested forging a new identity. One of them, Lynda Glennie, wondered in the *Falkland Island Newsletter* if the Kelpers "would serve themselves better if they spoke more of being proud citizens of the Falkland Islands and less of being British."

To do that they would need to admit that they are a hybrid culture and not only "British," whatever that means, which is unlikely to happen. The Falkland Islanders see themselves as British as the six o'clock news from London. As cottage pie. As the Union Jack. As Land Rover rallies with men and women on horseback cheering about something eight thousand miles and a hundred years distant. They have long looked eastward for salvation, never westward to their closest shore. One Falkland Islander explained to me that they were never a part of Patagonia, that they split off from the super continent of Gondwana millions of years ago. He failed to note that South America was part of the super continent, too. In his mind, the Falklands reassuringly kept their distance from South America through the eons, leaving me to imagine the islands floating unmoored and semi-delusional, no place more separate from its geography than this place.

Meanwhile, the very thing that makes the Falklands unique is dying. The population of Camp is aging—the 2012 census showed that 75 percent of the population now lives in Stanley and only 13 percent lives in Camp, a barely higher percentage than the remainder who live on the military base. At Goose Green, Adrian looked rather wistfully at the empty auditorium where eighty or more people would gather during "Sports Week," in late February. A year would go by between seeing one another, but for the week, there would be steer riding (discontinued because it's too dangerous) and horse racing (much of it takes place in Stanley now); and their solitary lives would be reaffirmed by the sense of community they forged over that week. Now Sports Week lasts all of four days at most and people see each other all the time (translation: too much) in Stanley. "I give it another decade," he said. "It'll be gone."

Is it the blood sacrifice of the English soldiers that makes the Falkland Islanders who they are? Is it a referendum? A stamp? Is it letters painted on a building? Looking at the diddle dee covered landscape and the stone runs, I wonder if the Islanders ever discern a gaucho on his horse skulking quietly by, his ghost shimmering in the incessant wind, as sullen at being erased from the island's heritage as he was in life at not being paid by Louis Vernet.

*

My landlady, an octogenarian named Kay, says that if there's anything going on for Guy Fawkes Day, it would be at Surf Bay. I ask if it's within walking distance. About an hour and twenty minutes, she says. An hour and twenty minutes walking at night in the Falklands doesn't sound safe or practical to me, with Land Rovers, the Islanders' preferred vehicle, racing by. I tried to walk out the other day to the closer Gypsy Cove, past countless windows with photos of Margaret Thatcher and signs proclaiming, "Our Islands, Our Choice," but hail started coming down, and when I faced the wind, the force of it left me breathless and red-faced.

On Guy Fawkes Night, I dine alone at the Malvina House Hotel (named after a nineteenth-century woman named Malvina, *not* a nod to the Argentine name, Malvinas) on blackened toothfish with Asian slaw and Chilean sauvignon blanc. Facing the Bay and the government house, three flags snap in the wind: the Malvina House flag, the Union Jack, and the flag of the Falklands, a Union Jack in its corner, a massive sheep standing on a patch of green on top of an old sailing ship, a logo beneath proclaiming, "Desire the Right."

A young woman at an adjoining table stands and throws down her napkin. "If there's one thing I have no patience for, it's racism," she tells the two young men dining with her, then she dashes from the restaurant for a furious smoke, pacing away her outrage. In this way, at least, the Falklands have changed with the times, much like the former British Empire itself.

Among the fewer than 3,000 Falkland Islanders, you can find now living among them 259 St. Helenians (another legacy of the British Empire, the last home of Napoleon Bonaparte, off the coast of Africa, its citizens making their way to the Falklands for employment), 140 Chileans, and 89 others. I've seen some evidence of these others during my stay.

Kay, who lives in the house in which she was born, one of the original settlement houses in Stanley, has a couple of third-culture grandchildren, her son married to a Thai woman. And one day, looking for a little variety in my meals, I hike up a hill in the wind and rain to a place called Shorty's that's been recommended, only to discover that it's run by a family of Filipinos. I react as though I've run into my own countrymen, chatting with the clerk in Tagalog, telling her of my travels to her country, my Filipino wife, my own third-culture kids.

Ezequiel enters the Malvina House restaurant just as I'm leaving, and we agree to see if there's anything going on in town tonight. Back at Kay's, I enlist Adam, the only other boarder at Kay's, in the hunt for Guy Fawkes. Adam is a medical student from London, on an internship here as part of his studies. Bedecked in lip and tongue piercings and something approaching a mohawk, his father Indian, his mother Polish, he describes himself as a "royalist," and says that those who are not are a distinct minority. A proud Londoner, he even danced in the official opening of the London Olympics.

That evening after dark, Ezequiel, Adam, and I walk along the darkened streets of Stanley, looking for anything resembling a bonfire, but finally wind up in the Victory Bar and, in lieu of a celebration, we clink our pints of Longdon Pride, two of us as foreign as Guy (originally, Guido) Fawkes himself. "I don't feel at all foreign here," Adam tells us. "I just feel like it's somewhere I don't know." The Falkland Island accent he finds unusual, difficult to pin down, but that's all. Perhaps a little like an Australian accent or New Zealand accent, or maybe just something from the West Country.

On the way back to Kay's, Adam tells us what it's like to sit on Primrose Hill on Guy Fawkes Night and watch the fireworks all over London. And then he looks up in the sky and points out the Southern Cross. "Can you see it?" he asks. I try, but I'm not sure I can. I just see stars, more or less indistinguishable from one another.

Mr. Chen's Mountain

From afar, Mr. Chen's mansion resembles a mosque with a gold dome, but on closer inspection has the look of a national treasury, its windows gleaming gold. Or a palazzo crossed with the Reichstag as imagined by a 1960s mafioso in Vegas. Its vast grounds are filled with Italianate statues crafted out of jade, marble, granite, and other stone. Roman soldiers on horseback rear with spears from the rooftop, while maidens in togas pour liquid from jugs. A statue of an American soldier, machine gun in hand, guards the side gate to the grounds along with a more traditional Chinese demon and a statue of a pudgy cop.

"Most Chinese would think his place is great—because it's so unexpected," says my friend Huang Li, who is serving as my translator over the next few days (both Huang Li and Mr. Chen are pseudonyms). "Even if it was in the middle of Shenzhen, we would think it's quite special."

This is my second time to Mr. Chen's. A year and a half earlier, I visited with a group of writers from around the world at the invitation of Li and the university where she's a professor. Most of my colleagues were amused by Mr. Chen's mansion and impressed by his hospitality, but my sense of righteous indignation was too easily triggered by Mr. Chen's excesses, as I saw them: five enormous padauk tree trunks, each twenty to thirty feet high, strung up behind his mansion. Shellacked and gleaming, inscribed with Chinese characters, they looked like giant slabs of beef jerky, and they dated, according to Mr. Chen, about two thousand years earlier, from the same era as the lines he had carved into the side of the largest, which proclaimed in Qin Dynasty script, "The King of the Padauk." He admitted that there's almost no way to save the forest they came from because China wants wood from around the world and, if he didn't buy it, someone else would. As he saw it, the trees had already been cut down, so he might as well buy them as a kind of aftermarket act of preservation.

At dinner one evening, he told us that he had considered purchasing an endangered pangolin for us to eat (you have to go farther and farther into the mountains to capture them, he said), but had reconsidered because he thought we would be sensitive about this. The kicker for me was discovering in front of our guest bungalows five enormous trees, which I identified as the endangered *Podocarpus costalis*, a tree that only grows on one island in the northern Philippines and a few islets in Taiwan. I've seen these slow-growing trees in their natural habitat, and I know someone who helped foil a smuggling ring that was trying to spirit some of the trees out of the Philippines to be sold to rich Chinese businessmen like Mr. Chen, who see them as bringers of good fortune. I asked Mr. Chen about these trees, musing that they must be worth at least $100,000 each. Yes, he told me with pride. He had purchased them for exactly that: $100,000 each, a bargain, but now they were worth $2 million all together. He claimed he had purchased them in Japan, not the Philippines. Perhaps, I thought—but then someone from Japan must have stolen them first.

Li recalls a saying: if you spend a day in China you can write a book; if you spend a month, you can write an article; if you spend a year, you can't write anything. The same can probably be said for America, where I've lived for most of my life: it baffles me more than ever the older I get. Somehow, the people with the least experience of a country tend to have the most opinions about it. The same is true of individuals: we tend to judge most heavily those who we know the least. The richer or more famous, the less we know them. "Fame is a form, perhaps the worst form, of incomprehension," Jorge Luis Borges once wrote.

*

My sense of incomprehension drove me back to Mr. Chen's, because I knew that my first impressions could not be correct, that there had to be more to him than his unabashed acquisitiveness. I had been under the impression, as were some of my colleagues, that Mr. Chen was a robber baron who had made his money raiding the forests of Vietnam and Myanmar or some such shady dealings. Mr. Chen certainly has a love of rare hardwoods. Entering his front door into what we might call the Great Hall of the Person, one feels like Jack stealing into the giant's lair: the room is lined with hardwood chairs that could comfortably seat a hippopotamus. At the end of the hall, near the grand staircase, one sees not the goose that lays the golden eggs, but a peacock as tall as a man, its plumage a snarl of knotted roots, a carving that any robber baron from whichever century and nationality would be proud to own.

His gold Rolex, his titanium Samsung phone, and his penchant for constantly pouring his guests Hennessy cognac from a bottle that costs $1,500 all add to the general air of ostentation around him. By his own estimate, he's spent $46 million on liquor over the last thirty years, which is $16 million more than the cost of his mansion. But the clothes he wears are serviceable, frumpy, even, his shoes nothing fancy. While he was not educated beyond high school, he reveres the Chinese classics. One promenade is devoted to scenes from *Dream of the Red Chamber*, and other Chinese cultural treasures are well represented on his grounds. Inspirational poems adorn the outside walls of the compound, so that strolling villagers might stop and read a classical verse to better themselves:

You plant some flowers and they never bloom. You plant a willow randomly and then it gives a lot of shade.

In the mountains, there are straight trees, but in the world there are no straight people.

His voice is soft as he stops to recite this one day as we stroll along the street that runs through his property and across a bridge over a canal to his ancestral village. "He actually knows them very well," Li says. I'm sure he's studied them—perhaps they were his touchstones of human behavior as he made his ascent. We in the West have our equivalents:

The best laid plans of mice and men often go awry.

Trust everybody but cut the cards.

We wind around the pond he widened and stocked with turtles, past the park he made for the people ("The New Rural Happy Garden"), which, he says, is packed in the summer with people playing cards and chess, but it's not now. There are plenty of honking geese, barking dogs, and sunning turtles, but few people. His ancestral home, a crumbling yellow brick structure overgrown with weeds, sits with equally dilapidated houses along a concrete slab of a road. I'd love to speak to some of the villagers to get their impressions of Mr. Chen, but there's no one around except for a farmer working in the middle of a muddy field some distance away. Does he view Mr. Chen as a favorite son, or as some alien who's landed in their midst in a giant spaceship?

The unavoidable comparison, clichéd as it might seem, is that Mr. Chen resembles in many ways *Citizen Kane*, and that his spectacular climb to wealth best fits the aspiration formerly known as the American Dream. His mansion, tacky as it might seem to a Westerner, is no more embarrassing than the incongruous homes of the nouveau riche in America, whether in Southampton, Atlanta, Beverly Hills, or Salt Lake City. Or the assorted Orientalist fantasies that inspired Western movie theatres in the early part of the twentieth century. So why not turn the tables? That Mr. Chen is fabulously wealthy and has kitschy taste is not in itself remarkable. What makes him remarkable is that he's not the Jed Clampett who moved to Beverly Hills but the Jed Clampett who returned home. He didn't have to do this. He could have gone to Shanghai or Beijing. He could have gone anywhere in the world. But he thinks Europe is strange, and he doesn't like America. He could have purchased a foreign passport and moved to Australia or Canada or the U.S., as many other Mr. Chens have done. A friend of his asked him to go in on an Australian island with him a decade ago for development as a tourist site, but he didn't want to go to Australia. His friend bought the island and has made a fortune. Mr. Chen's island is his mansion, floating over the toil of his ancestors.

*

Looking around Mr. Chen's village, it's not hard to imagine the poverty into which he was born. An older sister died at the age of three of starvation, a not uncommon fate during the period known as the Great Leap Forward. Beyond this, there's the familiar iconography of the rags-to-riches story: walking barefoot to school for seven kilometers, gathering and chopping wood to pay for tuition. As China's economic policies opened up, Mr. Chen saw his opportunity—not selling newspapers or shining shoes in Horatio Alger fashion, but dehusking rice. Borrowing 1,000 yuan from family members and a bank, he purchased some dehusking equipment and within six months had made back his investment.

Over my visit of several days, Mr. Chen shows me where that initial investment has led. He drives me (he likes to drive his black Lexus suv, modest by billionaire standards) to his international port with its many hectares of stacked cargo containers. But he doesn't enjoy visiting the port so much because there are no trees, and Mr. Chen, above all, likes wood, whether carved or au naturel.

At the port, we have lunch with various associates and his twenty-nine-year-old son, to whom he has given control of the port. He drives me to his headquarters in another nearby city, where a lot of people were sent during the Cultural Revolution. Li's own parents, both academics, were sent to the countryside to work, and Li almost had to go as well, but then "everything changed." This simple statement, "everything changed," accounts for the rise of Mr. Chen, and Li's own academic career, as well as the many high-rises in this port city and the empty lots that will soon no longer be empty.

In 1978, China adopted modernizing reforms to open its economy, protect private property rights, and facilitate international trade, which did in fact change everything for entrepreneurial souls such as Mr. Chen, but it also opened an income chasm between the rich and the poor that has widened ever since. Billionaires like Mr. Chen are the face of the new China: assertive, confident, and powerful. What the world sees now when we look at Mr. Chen and his compatriots is an enviable prosperity. Universities throughout the U.S. and elsewhere have benefited from the influx of thousands of Chinese students, who pay full international tuition and drive luxury cars through the streets of otherwise modest university towns, such as Iowa City, where Chinese students at the University of Iowa numbered over 2,000 in 2017—up from 537 in 2007. Likewise, the largest number of outbound tourists in the world come from China: 131 million in 2017, according to the China National Tourism Administration. But that's out of a population of nearly 1.4 billion people. What the world sees most often are the wealthy and middle-class Chinese, who can afford to send their children overseas to university and to travel widely. We rarely glimpse the shabbiness of the ancestral village, much less side by side with the stratospheric opulence of a mansion such as Mr. Chen's. Who builds a mansion amid squalor?

The Gini coefficient is a measure of inequality, quantifying the economic disparity between the wealthiest people in a given country and its poorest inhabitants. A country with a Gini coefficient of zero—were there to be such a place—would have perfect equality. As the number rises, so does the gap between the richest and the poorest. In 1980, when Mr. Chen and China both began their impressive rise, China's Gini coefficient was 0.3. In 2016, it stood at 0.47, according to the National Bureau of Statistics of China, making China one of the countries with the highest economic disparity in the world. (Of course, in the country's communist heyday, economic equality simply meant that people were equally poor.)

Since China's economic reforms, per capita income has unquestionably risen. Mr. Chen is one of China's 373 billionaires—the second-most of any country in the world, according to *Forbes* (the U.S. has 585, although the Hurun Report, the annual Chinese "rich list," puts China ahead of the U.S. with 819). He shares his wealth, in a sense, with the poor of his village through his public works, the mine he owns just up the road, and the servants he employs, but the incongruity of his mansion amid their shacks must seem a little strange to even those villagers who are proudest of him. It's as if Donald Trump decided to build a Trump Tower in his mother's fishing village of Tong on the Isle of Lewis in Scotland, rather than a golf course and resort among the environmentally protected dunes of Aberdeen. But then Trump has spent a total of 180 minutes on the island, and a cool 97 seconds in the cottage where his mother was born, according to Scottish media. If the Facebook page "Isle of Lewis DOES NOT Support Trump" is any indication, following in Mr. Chen's footsteps would not be a welcome move on Mr. Trump's part.

At Mr. Chen's HQ, one of his assistants shows me plans for a development nearby, complete with a private school for kindergarten through high school. Mr. Chen could have his name attached to any of these projects, à la Trump, but he chooses instead to bury it in the names of his enterprises. His full name is Chen Ze Hong, the last word, I'm told, meaning "big," and the school will be called Hong Xing School, Xing meaning "prosperous." It's a kind of anagrammatic credit he takes, prideful, clever, and reticent at once.

At both his port and on his mansion grounds, a statue of an eagle, it wings spread over a globe with China at its center, signifying, Li tells me, the feng shui concept of success, bears the inscription: "The eagle spreads its wings over the bright future." His name is included in this saying as well.

It's a feng shui world at Mr. Chen's. From the gardens to the placement of statues and furniture, Li tells me, his place is organized around its precepts. Over every doorway of his headquarters, an inspirational quote harnesses the power of Chinese tradition to maximize the possibility of good fortune:

You're having a great career.
Everything goes smoothly.
You're going to be safe.

Hardwood tigers and intricately carved roosters signifying prosperity roam the desks and display cases of his office. An artillery shell that used to hold poisonous gas, given to him by his old army mates, sits by his massive desk. It's inscribed with a saying: "You use one cannon and then you prosper." A canal running through his gardens is shaped like the royal scepter, the *ruyi*, which the emperors of old held, signifying "Everything as one wishes." Even the number and order of his children, boy-girl-boy-girl-boy-girl, according to Mr. Chen (and yes, he anticipates my question by telling me he was fined for having so many kids), signifies the word for "good." Everything is good at Mr. Chen's. Everything goes smoothly.

*

True to his name, everything is big, too. The mansion boasts a surplus of furniture, tea, liquor, statuary, and food. It's perhaps his humble upbringing, or the starvation death of his older sister, that makes him hoard. Mr. Chen is the billionaire equivalent of my grandmother, who lived through the Depression, and who left us when she passed away, among many useful things, many other objects she just wanted to store, such as a hundred or so tin pie plates beneath her stove. Somewhere, I'm convinced, Mr. Chen hoards pie plates, though they're probably made of titanium.

The largest conference table I've seen in my life, perhaps twenty-five feet long (I'm six feet tall, and you could fit at least four of me end to end) dominates a side room on the first floor that seems almost an afterthought. Meetings would more likely take place on the floor of meeting rooms, his third floor, or maybe even the floor above that, dominated by a strobe-lit karaoke hall. One day, we arrive back at the mansion to more hardwood furniture being unloaded, and Li and I both wonder where he's going to put it. The rooms are vast and empty and at the same time cluttered, their walls lined with big and ungainly furniture, like misfits at a school dance afraid of being the first out on the dance floor.

A tower rises by the main building of his mansion, reminding me of a medieval munitions tower I saw once in Florence, but this tower doesn't store gunpowder; it stores liquor, mostly cognac, and homemade rice wine made with special herbs that Mr. Chen swears by. Mr. Chen is obsessed with cognac. The French don't particularly enjoy their cognac—less than 3 percent of it was consumed in France in 2016. But it's a big business and a big status symbol in Mr. Chen's circles. I've seen entire duty-free stores in China that sell practically nothing but cognac. In 2011, half of Remy Martin's world exports, according to the *Wall Street Journal*, went to Asia, and three-quarters of that ended up in China. From the looks of it, half of that ended up in Mr. Chen's tower. Outside, the tower gleams like the rest of his mansion, its windows glowing gold. Inside, a narrow staircase leads past mold-covered and astringent-smelling walls to dank and dark rooms, like torture chambers filled with cauldrons of homemade liquor and stacked boxes of imported cognac—enough here, I think, to waterboard a planeload of cognac-averse French.

Still, as with China, the more you're around Mr. Chen, the less you can say of him with assurance. On one of his outside walls is written:

> You know the person, you know the face, but you don't necessarily know his mind.

My initial assumption, that he's simply another greedy *tuhao*, the Mandarin name for the nouveau riche, has started to erode slightly by the end of my first day. I ask him about the *Podocarpus costalis* trees in front of the guest villas that I was certain on my first visit had been smuggled from the Philippines. They're not *Podocarpus costalis* trees, he tells me in his soft voice, unperturbed (despite, Li tells me, my habit of firing questions at him like it's an interrogation). "They're Buddhist pine trees," he says. Sure enough, I've wrongly accused him. The trees are in the same *Podocarpus* genus, and look similar, but Buddhist pine trees are not the same, and they're not endangered.

Li says that her husband was similarly skeptical about Mr. Chen at first. Mr. Chen wanted her husband, an expert in tourism studies, to consult for him on a project. But the more Li's husband got to know Mr. Chen, the more he noticed a kind of thoughtfulness that wasn't simply about slapping down millions of yuan for dubious purposes—though there's inevitably some of that. Li's husband recently stopped Mr. Chen from purchasing a series of rejuvenation injections for $155,000. But vanity makes fools of us all. And Mr. Chen *did* fly in two helicopters for his son's wedding, which caused a bit of a stir in the county, but *come on*, we all lose our heads a little at weddings.

In other ways, Mr. Chen is methodical and rational (if not exactly always understated), and one of the things he was most interested in when building his mansion was whether it would have lasting value. The government gives him 200,000 yuan a year (US $31,000 at the time of my visit) to help maintain his mansion, which has been earmarked as a property with new cultural heritage status. Li thinks he must have had a lot of consultants helping him, for all the care taken to represent certain classical elements of Chinese culture and architecture, from the aforementioned statues drawn from classic literature to a walkway of giant figures from the Chinese zodiac and a replica of the Nine Dragon Wall from the Forbidden City. But Mr. Chen claims that 95 percent of the structure and the gardens were his ideas.

It's true that what seems at first wildly incongruous begins to make sense on closer inspection, with the exception perhaps of an Easter bunny statue with basket and button-down vest that looks like it came from the Garden Center at Walmart, stationed near the front gate. Even the donut cop and American soldier guards make a kind of sense. Mr. Chen figured that since he was building a Western-inspired structure, he should have some Western-style guards to ward away evil spirits. He doesn't believe in ghosts, he says, though he knows some people who claimed to have seen ghosts and they're all dead. And he once saw some green fire escaping from some graves. So it's best to keep your mind at ease, take the pressure off, especially if you've got the money to do it.

Not that money buys ease of mind, and not that Li or I or any-one else knows what goes on in Mr. Chen's mind. But he seems at ease. He doesn't have the coarseness Li and I associate with *tuhaos*, whether from southern China or South Carolina. And while he's constantly receiving visitors, and is at the center of many projects, there's a tranquility about him that Li remarks on several times. "The cloud is thin and the wind is light," is how she terms it.

Li, a dog lover, is particularly impressed that he always asks after her poodle—this after the poodle peed first thing in Mr. Chen's office. "He was very forgiving," she says. "Chinese men don't usually have time for animals. It took my husband several years to include the dog in any conversation."

Others seem to like him as well. He has unannounced dinner guests every night during my visit. One night, it's the county executive, four years younger than Mr. Chen. The county guy is constantly complaining and making fun of Mr. Chen to the delight of all the guests, which includes his thirty-something second wife. "There's too much liquor here," he complains at dinner, "and not enough veggies." And he says that the cigarette Mr. Chen offered him, the Double Happiness brand, is too cheap.

"They cost a hundred yuan," Mr. Chen says.

"They cost six," says the executive.

Mr. Chen could easily smoke more expensive cigarettes. One brand, 1916, sells for 8,500 yuan a carton, or about $1,220. But in the contemporary landscape, a certain modesty is perhaps prudent, as a lot of tall poppies are being cut by President Xi Jinping's much-touted anti-corruption campaign. It's best to offer your guests, especially if they're in government, the six-yuan cigs.

Through it all, Mr. Chen sits serenely, one arm across his belly, the other holding his cigarette aloft as though about to deliver an injection. There's a kind of ritualized hospitality that Mr. Chen practices artfully—serving Li and me the many dishes until my bowl and my plate brim with so much food I can't eat anymore, and then apologizing for the meagerness of the meal.

Behind the flashy signs of wealth and the false modesty—or culturally imposed, at least—Li suggests there's a kind of salt-of-the-earth quality that makes him a little vulnerable and insecure. He asked her once to set up his second son with a woman from a poor background (not someone of equal status, which would normally be the case), though he required that she be good at accounting. Li set him up with a graduate student, but the woman was bored by the young man, who, as is often the case, doesn't possess the canny intelligence of the father.

Sitting at his table is the one thing in my life I could have held over Anthony Bourdain, if I had ever met him. Twelve ornately carved chairs surround a massive table of some African hardwood (purchased, he says, premade at the Vietnam border), dominated by a large lazy Susan around which revolve feasts of preserved duck, daylily soup, steamed chicken, fish, fish-head soup, bok choy, fried rice, spare ribs, stuffed bean curd with pork, fried noodles with a delicious smoky flavor, and dense sticky rice cakes usually made for the Spring Festival. Nothing here has preservatives of any kind, or the controversial flavor enhancer MSG, only ingredients that are produced on his property: chicken, ducks, geese eggs, vegetables, even the oil in which they're cooked. He happily shows me the oil, stored in jugs in the back storerooms of his kitchen. With 20 percent of China's farmland contaminated by heavy metals, and the many scandals around recycled cooking oil from China's gutters, Mr. Chen's kitchen exemplifies a growing trend among those who can afford it, a somewhat elitist take on traditional back-to-the land movements.

There's no doubt Mr. Chen is a great host, despite the county executive's bellyaching, but how much more lavish a host might he have been several years ago before the corruption crackdown? Now, many older elites are scared, and luxury brands are just beginning to recover from a five-year slump, thanks to increased spending from China's wealthy millennials. In part, this is why Li asked me to give her and Mr. Chen pseudonyms: the situation in China has been tense, and no one wants to stand out. She's more concerned for Mr. Chen than herself, and while he's most likely not divulged anything that could land him in trouble with the authorities, she would rather err on the side of caution, as she would feel responsible if anything happened to him. I feel likewise about her. The various crackdowns and curbs in China have put a lot of people on edge.

A restaurant that Li likes in Shenzhen has seen its clientele plummet. A friend of hers went into the wine business at exactly the wrong time, importing inexpensive wine from Napa that costs under $10 in some parts of the U.S. In China, you'll pay 380 yuan (or $58) for it, which is a good value if only because, Li says, the number three means "value" and eight means "prosperous."

Mr. Chen clearly doesn't need Napa Valley wine to top off his prosperity or status. But he's not so rich as all that. "There are a lot richer people than me," he says. "In government."

"But they're all in prison or in hell," says Li with a smile.

Perhaps Mr. Chen's most lasting contribution (even more lasting than his mansion, which he boasts can withstand a magnitude 12 earthquake—not bad considering the highest earthquake ever recorded is 9.5) is his three-thousand-foot mountain. Cha Shan, or Tea Mountain, which covers three-quarters the area of San Francisco, he claims, would take fifteen days to explore (Mr. Chen seems a bit prone to exaggeration). His grandfather originally came from this mountain before there were any of the roads he's built to bring us there. Actually, it's the government's mountain, which he's renting for the next seventy years. He's only allowed to develop 5 percent of the land, which is still pretty substantial: by my calculations, 4.4 square kilometers of development. In his headquarters, he showed me five glossy books that Li's husband produced detailing every facet of the project, dubbed the Tea Mountain Leisure Scenic Spot (the concept, the actual plan and the sections of the park, the blueprint, the environmental impact, and the government regulations). On the early spring day we visit, lilac and other flowering trees and bushes are starting to bloom, and we've got the mountain to ourselves, though the summit is socked in with clouds, so he drives us only partway, to a muddy plane that's been cleared for a hotel with a view of trees that have been spared.

A lot of Chinese tourists, Li explains to me, don't want to simply view nature passively. A vacation on which you didn't do something wouldn't be a vacation. Mr. Chen's mountain theme park will be laced with helicopter pads to lift some of the ten million tourists he envisions annually up above the trees (again, Mr. Chen seems prone to exaggeration, as this lofty goal would bring him on par with the number of visitors annually to Shanghai Disneyland as well as the Great Wall of China); roads to bring them to their lakeside villas (the lakes created by the twenty dams he's in the process of building); and giant stones in these lakes so visitors can traipse across them.

On our way down the mountain, we stop at Mr. Chen's hideaway, a low concrete building with a red roof housing a small turbine for hydroelectric power and modest living quarters. Nestled between hills and a stream with the dam below, it has a view of a wide expanse of mountains. Not a car or another person is in sight. The caretaker, a middle-aged man in Wellies and a blue raincoat, lives here with a skittish dog, a telephone, a TV, and a cell phone. For food, he picks wild vegetables.

Mr. Chen's assistant, a woman in her forties named Chen Hong Mei (also a pseudonym), whose main function during my visit is to constantly pour us tea, remarks that if she lived here she wouldn't ever be able to speak again.

Mr. Chen bustles about the shack, covering a flaky old couch with a towel so we can sit. This is a place he sometimes brings guests, he says, as he shows off the inevitable stash of Hennessy XO and Martell—I'm assuming childhood friends or moguls like him, craving something simple without the burden of constant empire-building and flashy signs of success. Here there are only two dingy bedrooms, one for him and one for the caretaker, each furnished with a simple bed with a thin mattress, a chair, and a desk, remarkably not a splinter of padauk wood in sight. If this were his only property, you'd think he hadn't come so far from the life his grandfather led on this mountain. I ask Li to ask him if he likes it here because it reminds him of his childhood, but she thinks he won't really understand the question.

And she's right. He interprets the question as one of outcomes assessment. "I had been away from the village for thirty years, so I wanted to come back and do something to benefit my own people."

She tries another way. "Do you feel you belong here?"

He nods simply, *yes*.

Mr. Chen proceeds to tell us about the many and various delights of the place, the water in particular, its source so close to this dwelling that it's remarkably unpolluted. In the summer, you can take a bath in the little pool fed by a small waterfall behind the station, and anything cooked in this water, including a white vegetable Li has never heard of, will taste better, and you won't gain weight. He's even had the water tested.

"I could make a lot of money if I sold the water," he says, smoking his Double Happiness brand and drinking tea.

"Maybe you should," I say.

"I'm not selling," he says with a bluntness that's rare, as though I've asked him to sell a family heirloom.

*

Li, Hong Mei, and I venture out one evening from the mansion in search of someone to talk to who isn't employed by Mr. Chen. This is the first time Hong Mei has left the mansion in the month she's been in Mr. Chen's employ. Hong Mei is a fan of Mr. Chen, too. She worked for him ten years ago when he owned a porcelain business. She doesn't even know what her salary is going to be yet, but she says she's not worried. And he allows her to joke with him, even yell at him. When one night Hong Mei snaps a photo of him he doesn't like, she says, "What do you expect? I don't have an expensive phone like yours."

He smiles in response. "She's louder than I am."

The cloud is thin and the wind is light.

The village, as always seems to be the case, is deserted. It's as though all the villagers were killed when Mr. Chen's mansion landed on top of them. What kind of shadow does Mr. Chen's mansion cast upon the dilapidated houses, not much bigger than his guardhouse, with the requisite chickens pecking in the dirt and scrawny dogs barking? The poor are thin and light, too, like mirages. But if we find it striking that the economic disparity of China has grown exponentially over the past thirty years, perhaps we should examine, too, our own backyards, our own shining mansions casting shadows over the poor. The Gini coefficient for the U.S. is barely lower than China's, at 0.45, and by some accounts the two are nearly tied.

Though the U.S. has never pretended to be a land of economic equality, as China once did, the gaps between rich and poor, as practically everyone knows, have become as conspicuous as Mr. Chen's mansion. The top 1 percent, the Mr. Trumps, received 20 percent of America's income in 2015, compared to 11 percent in 1978, while in China, the superrich have gone from a 6 percent to a 14 percent share of national income. However, economists writing in *Global Inequality Dynamics* observed a "complete collapse" of the bottom 50 percent of American wage earners' income share between 1978 and 2015, while China's bottom 50 percent still earned a larger share of the country's income than the top 1 percent. Here, the kneejerk patriots among us might consider this an appropriate moment to break out into a chant of "U-S-A, U-S-A" We are still winning in our efforts to widen the gap between rich and poor.

*

On our stroll beyond Mr. Chen's compound, we spot a tiny store a few yards from his mansion, and I figure there must be someone inside. A man and a woman about Mr. Chen's age, seated on pink plastic chairs, are watching a news broadcast. The room is almost empty except for some modest piles of dry goods and basic household items packed on a glass counter, and on a few shelves behind it. The man is barefoot, hands behind his head, his feet propped on a couple of other pink chairs. He says they went to school with Mr. Chen, and Li asks if they keep in touch.

"He's so rich and we're so poor," the woman says.

The man, with a look of undisguised disgust, says, "He's busy and even I'm busy," and his legs climb a little high on the chair. He doesn't look busy, except in the sense of being suddenly unable to find a comfortable position for his legs. He tries placing them in the hole between the back and the seat, but he withdraws his feet again and tries a different position. Li points this out, unable to stifle a giggle as his feet keep climbing until he looks impossibly contorted in his attempt to pass for a man of leisure, his feet propped on top of the opposite chairs, his body almost a V. The first thing he sees when he leaves his small home is Mr. Chen's mansion. "We see it every day," he says, trying not to move his feet again. "So it's nothing special."

After our visit, Li can't stop laughing as we walk up the road to view Mr. Chen's quarry. Every few yards, she stops and can barely continue, overcome with giggles by the image of the man trying to prop his feet and get comfortable with his neighbor's impossible wealth. Hong Mei doesn't see what's so funny, while my own reaction is somewhere in the middle. I feel sorry for the guy, but I also recognize the ridiculousness of the situation, watching your neighbor's stratospheric rise with the knowledge that you have been left behind; that you can never catch up. And no matter how you feel about him, he's got the guards to keep out the hungry ghosts of his past, as well your envy, and all the world's bewilderment.

To the Rainforest Room

PART ONE

The Allure of Easy Cheese

I'd like to believe in Authenticity. Sincerely. I'm in favor of it. I sing its praises. Huzzah for Authenticity. But there are other times when I want to take that word "authentic" and just rip its white little belly open, tear out its offal-stuffed guts, and float it down the river on a burning pyre never to mention it again. Maybe stick its little helpmate "honesty's" head on a pike.

Maybe I should rephrase that.

Of course, I want everything in my life to be Authentic. I want to only eat Authentic Food and only have Authentic Experiences. When I travel, I want to travel authentically (hot air balloon, camel, steam railway). I want to meet Authentic People (family farmers, I think, are authentic, as are people you meet in the Polka Barn at the Iowa State Fair, members of lost tribes, and chain-smoking hairdressers named Betty). I want to think Authentic Thoughts.

Actually, Authenticity baffles me. I first wrestled with the notion some years ago when I was researching a book about a purported anthropological hoax. The Tasaday were "discovered" in 1971 in the southern Philippines leading an authentically Stone Age existence. They lived in isolation in the rainforest, had no metal or cloth except what had been given them by a local hunter, wore leaves, carried around stone axes and, most authentically, lived in caves. The Western world fell in love with them. Soon the Tasaday graced the cover of *National Geographic* and were the subject of countless breathless news accounts. No one could be more authentic than the Tasaday until 1986, when a freelance journalist from Switzerland hiked unannounced into their forty-five-thousand-acre reserve and was told through a translator that the famous Tasaday were nothing more than a group of farmers who had been coerced by greedy Philippine government officials into pretending to be cavemen.

My task was to unravel the mystery, to discover whether they were in fact a bald hoax or a modern-day version of our Pleistocene ancestors.

Before giving you the definitive answer, I'd like to interrupt this essay to bring you a word about Easy Cheese. If given a choice between the inauthentic (Easy Cheese!) and the authentic (cave-aged cheddar cheese from Cheddar, England, where it was invented a thousand years ago), I usually go for the authentic, unless of course I want Easy Cheese because sometimes that's what you want. This problem dates back to when I was in boarding school in 1974 and someone handed me a Triscuit (Original Flavor) topped with a vivid orange floret extruded from a can. What can I say? It tasted great. How can we hope to live authentically when we have been compromised by prior experience?

With that out of the way, we may proceed.

The Tasaday were neither Authentic Cavemen nor a hoax designed to fool the naïve public. They were, in fact, a poor band of forest dwellers whose ancestors had fled into the rainforest 150 years earlier to escape a smallpox epidemic. They became Pseudo-Archaics (a term used by Claude Lévi-Strauss) and lived more or less unmolested until they were "discovered" and made poster children for authenticity, chewed around for a while in the imaginations of the fickle public, then shat out onto authenticity's midden.

*

From time to time, I read sentiments like this: "For a few hours I lived in an alternative Africa, an Africa governed by a quiet glee and an innocent love of nature," and I think *your* quiet glee, buddy, *your* innocent love of nature. This sentence, by the way, is an authentic quote from an actual essay that appeared in a recent travel anthology. When I read it, I could get no further. I wondered what the writer thought he was doing experiencing his quiet glee in this alternative Africa. This sentimentalization of "Primitive Man" in harmony with nature seems akin to a hunter praising the pristine beauty of an elk head he's shot and mounted. The hunter can move but the elk can't. The authenticity tourist can and will depart the rainforest, leaving behind his tourist dollars and those irrepressibly authentic Africans twittering their gleeful songs on their kalimbas.

Nature declawed, stuffed, mounted. What, then, do we really want from the Authentic Destinations of our imaginations? And how do our perceptions of them differ from the Real Thing? When we think of an unspoiled place, how much do we need to strip away before we reach the desired level of authenticity? Strip Hawaii of its inauthentic fauna and you're left mostly with bats.

The idea of an authentic place implies an unchanging one, which also makes it an impossibility. I'm hyperaware of the aura of desperation and melancholy surrounding our common need for the Authentic, especially in regard to Place and People. Call it a sixth sense. If I were a superhero, this might be my special power, though it might also be my singular weakness, my kryptonite, which was, after all, the only thing that could kill Superman: a chunk of authenticity from a home planet he could barely remember. And no wonder— because neither he nor his home planet ever existed, except in our minds, where they continue to exist, and powerfully so.

And so I present for your further confusion, if not edification, three rainforests.

PART TWO

Lied Jungle: Omaha, Nebraska

Overlooking the second-largest waterfall in Nebraska, I wish that I could meet the plumber of this fifty-foot marvel. I asked to meet the plumber, but my request, I guess, was not taken seriously, and so I've had to make do with the director of the Henry Doorly Zoo, Danny Morris. I suppose I had some doubts about visiting one of the world's largest indoor rainforests before I showed up (yes, there *are* others). So what if a paradise tanager settles on a branch here? It's still Omaha outside.

Why would anyone go to the bother of bringing the rainforest to Nebraska? It's my theory that Nebraska has developed a severe case of landscape envy.

Arbor Day: invented by a Nebraskan.

The only man-made national forest (Halsey National Forest) is in Nebraska.

The word *Nebraska* originates from an Oto Indian word meaning flat water.

People of my generation will remember with fondness the weekly TV show *Mutual of Omaha's Wild Kingdom*, starring Marlin Perkins, which ran from 1963 to 1985 and gave most Americans their first exposure to the conservation movement. Perkins might not have been from Nebraska (though he was a midwesterner), but Mutual of Omaha, the show's proud sponsor, certainly was. It may be the most logical thing in the world that a state as mono-diverse as Nebraska would be infatuated with exotic flora and fauna. If the rainforest is the closest thing on earth to the Garden of Eden, to which we always hold out hope for our eventual return, Nebraskans may simply be looking for a shortcut.

Perhaps that's what drove the Henry Doorly Zoo's former director, Lee Simmons, to bring the rainforest to Omaha. Simmons had traveled to many rainforests around the world because a zoo such as Henry Doorly typically has a research component to its mission. In fact, in the actual disappearing rainforest of Madagascar, the zoo's staff and interns have discovered twenty-one previously unknown types of lemurs. One day, Simmons and others, including Danny Morris, taped two whiteboards together, set a perimeter, and started drawing things they'd like to have in their rainforest, including of course, the waterfall and a swinging bridge, de rigueur in any rainforest worth its mist.

Yes, it was planned, and yet planned to look unplanned, so that you might experience the rainforest as authentically as possible without the fear of lawsuits. In the jungle you hardly know what is in front of you and then you turn a corner and see a waterfall or monkeys in a tree. Simmons wanted to replicate that sense so that you'll never be sure what you'll find. Yes, of course, it's simulated, but at the same time "accurate." Simmons sent his "tree artists" to the Costa Rican rainforest. "You could tell the difference when they got back," Morris says. "Their trees were a lot better."

Consequently, in the Lied Jungle there are no surprises, and yet everything is surprising.

The white noise of water cascading from the waterfall is designed to mask the shrill voices of schoolchildren on their outings, as well as the many life-support systems required by the ninety or so subtropical species living within its 1.5 indoor acres. The eighty-foot tree in the center of the rainforest, cutting through its various levels, is made of polyurethane-reinforced concrete and is hollow, acting as a giant air duct, recirculating warm air from the ceiling of the eight-story-tall rainforest in the winter and venting it in the summer. The paths, a mixture of dirt and rock wool, which acts as a stabilizer, are rototilled. Walk up an artificial cliff to Danger Point, lean against the bamboo fence, and it wobbles to give the impression that it might give way at any minute. It won't. The bamboo is set on steel pegs.

Gibbons, hidden in the foliage, hoot like kids. Scarlet macaws perch on palm logs beside the epoxy tree they've vandalized by chewing on its branches. Bats fly free in the building, and arapaima, grown from twelve inches, loll in their pools, resembling manatees.

All of it seems authentic in most respects but happily inauthentic in others. At 6 p.m. or so, when the zookeepers open the doors of the holding pens, the animals are there waiting patiently to go in for the night, clocking out, as it were, for supper. And no one's threatening to put a road through Lied Jungle. No one's mining for gold. If we lost as much of the Lied Jungle today as we will of the Amazon, the Lied would be gone by tomorrow. And that, of course, is a large part of the point.

"You can watch all the National Geographic and Discovery Channel you want," Morris says as we pause in front of a curtain fig with its labyrinth of roots that kids can climb through. "But you need to smell it, hear it, and feel the heat. When you put all that together, it makes a more lasting memory."

So what if this tree is in finely fitted segments that are keyed for easy removal and reassembly?

Morris frets that, in the age of Google when everything is at our fingertips, nothing is actually touched, and the idea of the rainforest will become ever more remote to Nebraskans, as will the notion of anything authentic at all. He's noticed fewer field trips from the local schools. (Morris himself started at the zoo over thirty years ago as a volunteer Explorer Scout.) And the zoo staff has been talking recently of adding to the exhibits a Nebraska farm because so few Nebraskans have ever set foot on a real farm.

But doesn't the word *authentic* lose all meaning if applied too liberally? What is an authentic cup of decaffeinated coffee? An authentic polyester suit? What are the essential properties of an authentic family farm? An authentic family farm would seem to need—now I'm just speculating here—a family running it, rather than the well-meaning staff of a zoo. But that might just be me.

Morris and I walk effortlessly from the rainforest canopy to the riverbed, across three continents, passing pythons and other creatures we wouldn't likely see in the real rainforest and would actually hope to avoid. In this rainforest, the one thing you must not do is step off the path, but if you do step over the little rope you might just turn a corner and find something completely unexpected: an EXIT sign above a garage door big enough to drive a truck through.

We walk across a bat guano minefield, through a smaller door next to the garage door, and come upon a wide tunnel ringing the complex that seems straight out of a James Bond film. We've dropped into an entirely different realm now. The green EXIT sign, the garage door, and suddenly we're confronted by—what? No evil henchmen, no jungle drug lab, but wading pools, animal toys, a reverse-osmosis system, and doors that seem like metaphysical portals: one says, "South America," another, "Malaysia." It's here in these rooms, the holding pens for the animals, that the pretense of authenticity drops away. These rooms are the Lied Jungle equivalent of the actor's dressing room. Morris enters respectfully, not wanting to encroach on the animals' downtime, but also concerned that a François' langur monkey might snatch my glasses. The black monkey with its bulging abdomen regards me from its wildness, sees that I am of no importance to its world, and ignores me. Somehow, this moment of disregard strikes me as the most authentic of the day.

PART THREE

Arajuno Jungle Lodge: Ecuador

From a motorized dugout canoe on the Arajuno River, I see a mostly unbroken screen of foliage on either bank. A woman does laundry on one muddy bank while her naked toddler squats and plays. A couple of men run a machine in the water, dredging for gold. They can make up to $150 a day for about six grams. The river flows swiftly after several days of rain. A young man perched in the bow of the canoe, barefoot, wears a muddy T-shirt and shorts. He sees the same scene every day, yet he seems mesmerized by it, as though the river is someone he has recently fallen hopelessly in love with, or perhaps he's daydreaming of his real beloved, waiting for the right spot where he can get a signal on his cell phone and text her. We pass a young man in the river fishing with a net. Ten years ago, before my companion in the canoe, Tom Larson, arrived, the man might have used dynamite to fish instead.

A wheelbarrow and two giant bamboo saplings that Tom is donating to the community of Mirador for erosion control lie in the canoe beside us. The canoe is the local taxi service, so we're also joined by a woman in her twenties who has been to the market. We pull up to a heavily forested bank—her stop. The woman, a Kichwa Indian like most of the locals here, gathers her belongings: a backpack, a large white sack, a live chicken she dangles by its ankles in front of her. Two children and another woman descend the fern-lined embankment to give her a hand, one child reaching into the canoe and grabbing the real treasure: a liter bottle of Coke.

We pull away again and soon pass a sight that seems nearly as incongruous as a garage door in the middle of a jungle. A billboard protected with a thatched roof sits in a mostly denuded spot on the sandy bank, a few desultory banana plants growing beside it. The billboard shows a local official nicknamed Ushito, smiling broadly and giving the thumbs-up sign. Behind the trees, barely out of sight and parallel to the river, bulldozers have recently carved out a muddy track that will someday be a road connecting indigenous communities that until now have been connected mainly by the river. The road is one of Ushito's campaign promises. And today is Election Day. In jungles like this, roads tend to lead to deforestation, formerly inaccessible tracts of old growth being too tempting for illegal loggers to ignore. But labeling them "illegal loggers" makes them sound foreign. For the most part they're locals, though the buyers they're selling to are not.

When we reach Mirador, invisible from the shore, the bamboo plants are unloaded with the help of the canoe's pilot and a couple of local boys. Tom, wearing his typical uniform—Arajuno Jungle Lodge cap, T-shirt, cargo pants, and sturdy rubber boots—instructs the men in Spanish what to do with the bamboo. The fastest-growing bamboo in the world, these saplings, already seven feet tall, will grow into bamboo Godzillas in a short while.

In his midfifties and wearing wire rims, Tom speaks softly and has the bearing of someone who has nothing to prove but can easily prove anything he wants to prove, a lifetime of conservation knowledge always at the ready. When Larson first landed in the area in the late '90s and purchased the eighty-eight hectares that became Arajuno Jungle Lodge (sixty-five hectares of primary growth and the rest secondary), a multihued paradise tanager landed on a nearby branch, and Tom took this as an omen. This is paradise, he thought. A former U.S. National Park Service employee and Peace Corps official with a master's from the University of Idaho in environmental interpretation, Tom Larson has been trying to balance the books between paradise and "progress" ever since. Over time, the Arajuno Jungle Lodge has transformed from a personal project to save a small swath of rainforest, to an eco-lodge, and now a nonprofit foundation dedicated to helping the locals earn a living while not destroying their birthright in the process.

Hence, the fast-growing bamboo that we've transported to Mirador, which not only controls erosion, but can be used as building material and its young shoots eaten. Several days before my arrival, some university students from Canada and the U.S. planted this same variety of bamboo on the western edge of Tom's eighty-eight hectares as a clearly visible boundary. "You'll probably be able to see it from satellites when it's grown," he says. His property abuts the Jatun Sacha Reserve, two thousand hectares of rainforest, where on any given day you can find people cutting down trees (and through which cuts yet another road, this one eight kilometers long, despite a toothless legal ruling saying it shouldn't be there). Tom's bamboo boundary is in part to let everyone know quite clearly that this is Tom's part of the forest. No one, no one local at least, would cut one of Tom's trees.

In the Make-of-It-What-You-Will Department: Tom Larson was born and raised in Omaha, Nebraska.

The center of Mirador is deserted when we arrive after a short hike along a muddy and tangled path. Tom thinks perhaps they've formed a *minga*, a work party, and are off helping someone build or paint something. A field of grass defines the place, surrounded by a sparse and unevenly spaced ring of huts, some thatched, some roofed with tin. Tom points out the local school. A couple times a year, a group of students from the U.S. comes to Mirador and adjacent Santa Barbara to do projects. This year the students painted the school. Tom leads me across the field to check on some solar panels languishing inside the small building. The residents used the panels, donated by a Spanish group several years ago, to power their cell phones, but the storage batteries have since died.

Along a muddy path cutting through waist-high grass, we hike back to the river and hitch a ride in a canoe across to Santa Barbara, where Tom wants to show me the results of the aquaculture project he initiated. Tom started the project because, well, the dynamite blasts were "scaring the shit" out of the ecotourists at his lodge. First rule of ecotourism: keep dynamite blasts to a minimum.

He asked the locals what it would take to stop them from blasting the river, and they said they'd stop dynamiting the fish out of the water if they had their own supply of fish. So Tom, in partnership with the Peace Corps and with help from local residents, built twelve fishponds in four communities. The Arajuno Jungle Foundation and the Peace Corps supplied the first five hundred fingerlings of *cachama* (a native fish) and tilapia (the ubiquitous supermarket fish), plus two one-hundred-pound bags of fish food. After that, the communities were on their own. Tom sent out word that anyone caught fishing with dynamite would never get assistance of any kind from Arajuno. Dynamite fishing has been reduced by 90 percent, he claims. Additionally, the Arajuno Jungle Foundation (whose board is made up exclusively of Nebraskans) built the water system for the ponds with Peace Corps assistance and built another system to bring water to the village.

When you imagine a rainforest pool, it's almost certain that you do not imagine the fishponds of Santa Barbara. These utilitarian holes have been gouged between huts with planks and muddy paths running between them, pvc and hoses snaking all around. One woman wears a T-shirt with the smiling face of Ushito! She scatters fish food on the still surface of her pond, and hundreds of two-month-old fingerlings swim to the surface—all tilapia, because cachama fingerlings cost more and are somewhat more difficult to care for. The people in Santa Barbara don't really seem to worry that cachama are indigenous (and thereby authentic) while the tilapia are not.

A couple of ponds look dirty. One that wouldn't hold water has been turned into a muddy volleyball court. Another is empty because its drunken owner fell out of his canoe and drowned.

In the center of the village, we sit with a few local men and chat. The most talkative is Jaime, who has a reputation as a drunk, but he's a good-natured drunk. He offers us *chonta*, the red palm fruit that appears once a year, about the size and shape of a Roma tomato, and begins thanking Tom profusely for helping them with their fish and saying how proud he is of his community that they have stopped dynamiting the river. Jaime, who appears to have been swilling local hooch all afternoon, gives me the thumbs-up sign. So do his companions. "Ushito!" they all yell in unison.

Back at the Arajuno Jungle Lodge, I'm enjoying an afternoon of quiet glee, swinging innocently in a hammock overlooking the river. Tom flips through a copy of the New Yorker I brought with me. He asks if I'd like to watch Pink Floyd's The Wall sometime this week. Sure. Why not? That's what I came to the rainforest for. The guide who brought me here from Quito, Jonathan, who grew up in Ecuador, but whose parents are American, lolls like me in a hammock.

"You hear that?" Tom says.

At first I don't, but then a faint whine separates itself from the birds and the river. "That's the sound of progress," he says.

Jonathan looks up, listens, and says, "There's three of them at least," meaning three men working chainsaws somewhere in the forest.

"I used to stop what I was doing when I heard chainsaws and investigate," Tom says, bringing beers for all of us to two long picnic tables near the hammocks. "But why should I put my head on the chopping block when they're not going to do anything anyway?"

By "they," he means his neighbor and much bigger reserve, Jatun Sacha. By "chopping block," he means getting shot or blown up. He's found dynamite on the hood of his car before. Last year, a park guard was shot. A bullet grazed his head and, when the police came to arrest the gunman, they found themselves in a standoff with the man's many armed supporters, most of them from Santa Barbara. The police turned and ran.

"I've gone to Jatun Sacha how many times?" Tom says. "If you go on any Thursday they're cutting down trees to sell at the bridge in San Pedro on Friday. I've told Alejandro, 'I don't even mention this to you anymore because you never do anything.' 'I don't do anything,' he says, 'because I can't do anything. The police don't do anything. The Ministry of the Environment doesn't do anything.'"

Alejandro, whom I've met, is the director of Jatun Sacha. With his shoulder-length hair, thin mustache, and tired eyes, he looks a bit like Don Quixote, which is probably not an entirely inappropriate comparison. Jatun Sacha sold the right-of-way for an oil pipeline to run through the reserve and, in exchange, two community internet centers were constructed that allowed eighteen people to finish high school. He's doing the best he can. And by "the best he can," I mean he wins Pyrrhic victories.

But if the notion of compromise isn't native to the rainforest, it has certainly taken hold here, kicking notions of authenticity from the nest. The tourist who clings desperately to the latter might console himself briefly with the idea that authenticity is a man-made concept (like Easy Cheese!). Before this was a rainforest, it was an ocean. Was it more authentic then? Notions of authenticity themselves are a kind of invasive species.

In any event, there's no way to keep commerce and its insatiable appetites at bay for long. A new international airport in Tena, fifteen minutes from Arajuno, is slated to open soon. Ushito's road will continue being built across the river but won't likely be finished before the next election. Once the road is complete, Tom contends, the forest will go.

"If I were to oppose that road," Tom says, "my name would be mud around here." Instead, he effects what positive change he can. His teeming fishponds are stocked with giant cachama and *handia*, as well as native turtles he plans to restock in the river. And Arajuno bustles with projects for the community: a ceramics workshop, a workshop to train rainforest guides, a project to create medicinal plant gardens for indigenous communities. Even a French chef trains local women to cook meals using native plants for ecotourists at the various lodges in the region. My imagination takes flight and I envision pan-seared cachama with a chonta ragout. In this way, it's not just bellies that get fed but fantasies, too, what we might call the

Paradise of Cell Phone Coverage for the people of Santa Barbara, and what we might call the Paradise of Accessible Inaccessibility for the rest of us. A Paradise of Roadless Places with a way for us to enter. A Paradise of Contradictions.

PART FOUR

The Greater Blue Mountains World Heritage Area
Rainforest and Scenic Railway: Katoomba, Australia

The *Indiana Jones* theme song welcomes me to my third and final rainforest, as I and about sixty other tourists, the largest contingent from China, crowd into a funicular that is open on all sides and covered with a green, cage-like mesh. To gain access to the Greater Blue Mountains World Heritage Area Rainforest and Scenic Railway, I purchased a ticket in the gift shop that entitled me to plunge, via the steepest funicular railway in the world, down to the forest floor and ride the Scenicender, the steepest cable car in Australia, back up whenever I have seen enough to warrant the price of admission. And that will be whenever that invisible gauge in me that craves authenticity hits full.

I consider this a Bonus Rainforest, like an offer in which you buy two rainforests and get the third for free. Truthfully, I stumbled upon it. An hour ago, I was in suburban Australia, on a pleasant and tame street in the town of Katoomba, in a house overlooking a garden. But now I am caged and strapped into my seat on my way down the side of a mountain. In the spirit of adventure, I'm even wearing my Arajuno Jungle Lodge souvenir cap.

I'm visiting Katoomba on a retreat of sorts, the nature of which isn't important, except that it involves spending most of my time indoors, chatting amicably with a group of Australian writers, most of whom ask me daily if I've had the chance "to take a stroll down the path to the overlook." Not one of them told me there was a rainforest there. You'd think this was something one ought to mention.

Admittedly, one of them did describe it as "like the Grand Canyon but with trees."

Until now, Katoomba has seemed like another tourist town the likes of Park City, Utah, or Asheville, North Carolina, with sloping streets, pleasant houses, grocery stores, boutiques, restaurants, and quaint architectural landmarks, in this case the grand Carrington Hotel, built in the late 1800s. To learn why it has the feel of a tourist town, go down Katoomba Street to Echo Point Road until you find yourself, almost without warning, facing an overlook as impressive as any in the world. Suburbia suddenly ends and a kind of prelapsarian fantasy begins as you gaze out upon seemingly endless miles of mountains, replete with rainforests and waterfalls, and the giant stone pillars known as the Three Sisters. It is indeed like the Grand Canyon but with trees.

If someone had just uttered the magic word *rainforest*, I would have dropped everything to experience its majesty.

The exhibit, if we might refer to nature that way, can be found at the end of the funicular ride, where, upon disembarking, I find myself on a boardwalk surrounded by railings to protect the flora and fauna from me, as one sign admits. The forest floor is dominated by gum trees and a Chinese tour group with a harried, flag-waving guide who wants everyone to stay together. I want to get away from them, not because they're Chinese, but because they're human, and one of the reasons I go to the rainforest is to get away. I don't want to hear Chinese or English or French spoken. If in Ecuador, I want to hear the three low whistles of the undulated tinamou, a floor-dweller the size of a pheasant, answered by the longer and higher whistle of the little tinamou. If in Omaha, I want to hear the roar of a fifty-foot waterfall drown out hordes of schoolchildren. Here, I'd like at least a kookaburra with its almost stereotypical jungle call, the avian equivalent of *Ooh ee ooh ah ah, ting tang walla walla bing bang*.

I run down the boardwalk, pursued at a brisk pace by the Chinese. Signs along the path identify various plants, but I hardly have time to note them. I stop briefly at a blueberry ash, with its cluster of drooping white flowers, and also at a gray mound, a giant termite's nest, "home to a million termites or white ants." Ahead of me, a man speaks softly into his digital camera's microphone while jogging at a good clip and pointing the camera at the forest canopy. His efficiency and his lung capacity impress me, and I run after him just to see if I can keep up. His wife, also jogging, glances over her shoulder at me, seemingly alarmed, and I fall back. I would love to chat with them to ask why they're jogging as they film, how they think they'll remember this experience, but I'm too out of breath.

At a crossroads, one sign points to the Sceniscender, which will lift me away from this place and back to suburbia, but I'm not ready to be lifted. TO THE RAINFOREST ROOM, another sign proclaims, pointing in the opposite direction, and I think yes, "Tally ho! To the Rainforest Room!" I imagine a jungle glen, a stream, a twittering canopy in dappled light.

Ahead of me is an octagonal, open-sided building made of the kind of wood you'd build your back deck out of, with twelve benches and a trash can in the middle. I sit down on one of the benches across from three young Australian women and one man, taking a breather.

"I think she's pretty," one of the women announces.

"No, not at all," the man beside her says.

"I think she's pretty in a European way," she says.

"No, not at all," he insists.

A sound separates from the conversation—faintly in the distance, not a chainsaw, but a plane, its insect whine claiming the empty space it glides across.

The Australians stand up to leave.

"I'd come back here," one of the women says.

"Not me," says the man. "No toilets."

I spot, a little way up the path, a flag waving frantically, drawing closer.

Half an hour later, the Sceniscender lifts me and about fifty other people back to the familiar world. We ride up and out of the jungle—past the Three Sisters, past a defunct roller coaster that was built over the gorge but never officially opened—and are delivered directly into the maw of the inevitable gift shop. Here, I can purchase any number of didgeridoos, placemats, and coffee mugs decorated with aboriginal art, stuffed toy wallabies, and outback hats. I resist.

Stepping out into the parking lot, I find myself thinking about how often our idea of what's real differs from what's actually there. And about how certain concepts persist in our consciousness long after they've disappeared. When the Dutch killed the last dodo on Mauritius in the 1600s, the idea of the dodo did not cease to exist. It became the poster bird for all creatures that are too stupid to save themselves. Still, any loss over time becomes more bearable. I can't authentically experience a dodo, but I can imagine it. I can Google a dodo, and in this sense get closer to a dodo than most people did who were alive when dodos still existed. And though dodos no longer walk the earth, I saw a real dodo foot at the British Museum when I was eleven.

Maybe everything authentic eventually winds up an exhibit. Worse, maybe everything authentic eventually winds up depicted on a shot glass in a gift shop. Maybe the very idea of authenticity implies extinction. For the record, I'm *not* in favor of extinction. Here's one test: if you want to replicate it but can't, it's probably authentic. So maybe authenticity is something to be wished for, catalogued, but never owned. Something we can't quite pin down, but nevertheless yearn for. Something that, for a while anyway, can keep at bay the nightmare of a globe covered with polyurethane trees and inhabited by wild animals who clock out every evening.

Present

Rarely are all the members of my wife's far-flung family present—the last time was at the wedding of Margie's youngest sister and, before that, the death anniversary of Margie's father when all of us convened on her small city in Mindanao: the sister and husband from Adelaide, the brother and wife from Isabella Province, the sister and family in Toronto, and us, living in Iowa at the time. After each ceremony, we visited the family graveyard and washed the grave of Margie's great uncle, Datu Joseph Sibug, a Marcos-era congressman. Margie's mother remarked ruefully at the squatters in the graveyard who had been buried without permission, but with a kind of graceful resignation to the fact that, in the Philippines, no boundary is absolute. Shortly before Datu Sibug died, the story goes, while he lay in an intensive care unit in Mindanao, he appeared at a session of Congress in Manila for roll call. "Present," witnesses heard him say clearly, when his name was called.

To be present is to be counted, to be recognized and, perhaps for this reason, it's taken Margie nearly a year to leave our home in Iowa and join me in Singapore.

On our first visit together to Singapore, we rode in a taxi driven by a friendly man who informed us that the only thing wrong with Singapore was that there were too many Chinese (he meant those from the PRC, as he was of Chinese ethnicity himself) and too many Filipinos. Margie, who is half Manobo and darker than many Filipinos, often passes for African American or Jamaican, and she laughed at the man's remark, choosing not at that moment to be present in her Filipino skin. Sometimes it's easier that way—she grew up with the racism of fellow Filipinos who looked down on her for her dark skin, so this kind of remark was nothing new or particularly hurtful, at least on the surface. Like all such remarks, she banked it: a strike against Singapore to be catalogued with similar racist and xenophobic remarks she'd read on the website the Real Singapore. I suppose I could have and should have stepped up and said something to that cab driver, but I was suffering, as I sometimes do, from a mild case of "did he just say that?" And I wanted to stay positive, to ignore the moment. Who cares about a cab driver mouthing off? What was he to our lives? There are racist people everywhere.

Several years ago, I won an award that allowed me to live anywhere I wanted for a year. Teaching in Prague for part of the summer, I thought that I could hardly find anywhere lovelier to spend a year, but Margie, who was set to visit me, said, "Wait until I get there before you decide." On her first day in that city of confectionary architecture, a waitress refused to serve us. She didn't refuse in words, as she didn't speak English and we didn't speak Czech, but she laughed at us and wouldn't wait on us when we sat down. Scratch Prague off the list. So we spent the year in the Philippines, but even there, we had some trouble. While looking for apartments, the manager of one place asked where I was from. "America," I told her.

"Ah, that explains why you like the negra," she said.

Scratch that place off the list.

Undoubtedly, that Singaporean cab driver who said there are too many Filipinos in Singapore was partly responsible for the fact that Margie had yet to join me here. Subconsciously, at least, she agreed that Singaporeans don't need another Filipina in their midst. As a result, I lived for the first year in Singapore on my own, and the next six months with my two young daughters and our dog, Molly. But Margie and our cat (who's kept her company in Iowa) had yet to follow, her putative reason being that she needed a year in her job as a nurse before having the requisite experience to land a good job in Singapore. That was partly the reason but, in effect, we had switched allegiances. We joked that I was now probably more Pinoy than she, and that she was more American. One of the biggest exports of the Philippines is its people, "Overseas Foreign Workers," spread out in a great diaspora and sending remittances home to their families. Part of the reason I took my job in Singapore was to be closer to the Philippines. Meanwhile, in the ten years we had spent in Iowa, she made close friends, a lot of them Filipino émigrés and Fil-Ams.

Our American friends thought our arrangement was a bit strange, living so far apart. Even stranger that she could willingly separate herself from her children. But it *was* temporary, we reminded ourselves, though temporary kept becoming longer and longer. Even for our children this had been a good move, a further bonding between me and them. And in the international school where they were enrolled, their favorite subject was Mandarin, which suited me fine. If someone was going to insult us, I wanted at least someone in my family to understand the slight.

When Margie visited, we often went to Lucky Plaza, the slightly rundown shopping center that is a kind of Filipino enclave, full of Filipino grocery stores, places to send money home, and Filipino eateries, crammed on Sundays with Filipinos, many of them domestic helpers, on their day off. On these visits, in Margie's company, I relaxed in this otherwise tense city and felt almost at home. But I wasn't "Pinoy," and there were enormous and obvious differences between me and real OFWs, even though I regularly sent remittances home to Iowa for my Pinoy wife and American cat. We were more like exclaves of one another. Some separations, I know, are forever, but ours, I hoped, was temporary, and each time I retrieved Margie from Changi Airport, I willed the cab driver not to share his opinions on foreigners as we watched the city skyline unfold before us, like so many cheerfully wrapped presents, as yet unopened.

Celebrating Russian Federation Day with Immanuel Kant

Embrace Change

(Do You Have a Choice?)

The River Pregolya, known in Immanuel Kant's day as the Pregel, its waters calm and lily-padded, flows past tourists, Russians mostly, but also Polish, Lithuanian, and the occasional German, lounging at a café near an imposing red church, Königsberg Cathedral. The only survivor in this immediate vicinity from Kant's day, the church puts on a show by merely existing. In August of 1944, English bombers carried out two nights of raids on Königsberg. The buildings on the small island of Kneiphof on which the cathedral sits, once a warren of twisting medieval streets, were nearly leveled on the second night, the cathedral demolished, the hundred small children seeking refuge in its basement . . . *kaput*. What survived that night: the shell of the building and Immanuel Kant's tomb.

The cathedral's new spire, lowered by helicopter into place in 1994, exactly resembled the old spire, except for the molecules of which it was made, the hands that crafted it, and the crucible of history between the cathedral's 1335 dedication and the late twentieth century. Though the buildings that surrounded it have long ago vanished, the scene is pleasant if you restrict your gaze to the river, the cathedral, the other businesses along the Pregolya done up like actors at a Renaissance fair, and ignore the massive supermarket across the street, the "sex shop" with its flashing lights and dark windows, the apartment blocks of the same variety found all over the former Soviet empire, lined up like spectators in the cheap seats at a pageant.

Today is Russian Federation Day. I've come to what is now the Russian city of Kaliningrad for this and for Immanuel Kant, specifically because of his treatise, "Towards Perpetual Peace, A Philosophical Project," in which he attempted to convince the world of the late eighteenth century that we should replace classical law with "cosmopolitan law" and consider ourselves citizens of the world. Even at that time, the notion seemed a tad unrealistic, and none of his friends thought he would get far, but some admired his bravery for trying. Kant argues that all nations should be republics (though not necessarily democracies, of which he was skeptical) founded on three ideals: the freedom of all people as individuals, the equal application of laws to all citizens, and the equality of all citizens. He likewise proposed "universal hospitality," the right to move freely between states. Kant loved travel books, but he loathed change, and so it's a safe supposition that while he thought people should be able to move freely between states, he wouldn't have approved of what's transpired in his hometown: a case of states moving freely through people.

But I haven't ventured here to engage in pointless nostalgia for a dead philosopher's city that was destroyed before I was born. I *am* here for some of the ironies of the place: that the birthplace of the author of a treatise of perpetual peace hailed from a realm of total and merciless war. After World War II, the Soviets made Kant's city into a military zone forbidden to outsiders. When the Soviet Union's borders receded, Kaliningrad, renamed after one of Stalin's cronies, was retained by Russia, a region a little bigger than Connecticut, that never was Russian before (except for four years during Kant's lifetime when the Russians occupied Königsberg), and is now Russia's westernmost territory, surrounded by Poland and Lithuania. I'm here for Russian Federation Day, in a Kantian spirit, as a cosmopolitan, a citizen of the world.

The Russians do not see me that way. The Russian Consulate in Chicago gave me exactly a week's visa, no more, no less, and when I discovered two days before my trip that they had shortchanged me by one day, it wasn't the visa that needed to change, but my plans. Consequently, I spent a dismal afternoon in an Aeroflot office in Hong Kong, proffering a visa of a different sort, one that extends universal hospitality in its own special way, erasing almost all borders between nations.

SECOND MAXIM:
Be Skeptical of Everything You Read
(Except For This)

"Happy holiday," the ticket taker says at the entrance to the Kaliningrad Zoo. Formerly the Königsberg Zoo, the people of Kaliningrad "kind of inherited the zoo" in the words of a young guide at the town's tourist information center. The inheritance took place on April 8, 1945, when the Russians launched a surprise attack from two sides, led by "hero of the Soviet Union" Lieutenant Lopshin, who with his troops killed 30 and took 185 "Hitlerites" prisoner. If they were lucky, those prisoners survived the war and spent the next five years or so at hard labor, rebuilding the city they had helped destroy in the name of their leader. The animals fared no better than the Hitlerites. Only a deer, a badger, a donkey, and a wounded Hippopotamus named Hans survived. Hans lived many years beyond the war and became the zoo's symbol.

Today the zoo is filled with animals again, though the only cries are those of the peacocks and small children as they run in front of their parents. Spiderman encourages passersby to have their photos taken with him. A child has her face painted. A small tram ferries families around the wooded zoo and, amid all this gaiety, of a variety found in small municipal zoos everywhere, few signs of trauma persist. But neither are they ignored. Suitcase-sized placards dot the grounds, depicting the zoo as it was before the "inheritance," or directly afterward. One placard shows the main hall and restaurant of the zoo, the Gessellschafthaus from 1911, a group of women wearing hats the size of sombreros sitting on park benches beside conical hedges, and the same building in various stages of ruin and reconstruction, devoid of hedges and people after the war.

An enlarged photo of a woodcut from 1927 shows a couple viewing animals inside a barn-like structure, now rickety but still extant, its blue paint nearly stripped from its wooden sides. Its cages hold a macaque, and vultures, the macaque staring at visitors as though engaged in a chess match, and it's their move. Some visitors have pushed bananas through the bars of his cage, but he disdains these, and I remind myself that this is the zoo for the people of Kaliningrad, not me, and I need to leave my American objections out of this.

Two jagged slabs jutting out the ground, the height of a person, have been repurposed as art, artifact, stone tablets bearing not commandments but subtle cautions, Kantian values written in Russian on one slab, German on the other:

Logic, Freedom, "The thing in itself," Metaphysics, Reason, Worthiness, Self-Respect.

In his old age, Kant thrived on routine and lived his life by maxims he formulated after much thought and logical consideration, and from which he never wavered. As his maxims became more ossified, he and his friend, the learned English merchant Joseph Green, who also lived his life in this way, tried almost to outdo one another in how unwavering they could be with their maxims. When Kant missed an early morning meeting time for a country jaunt, Green took off in the carriage without him. Kant caught up with Green down the road and waved his arms wildly to get Green's attention, but Green never slowed down. Slowing down would have gone against one of his maxims. Kant was perhaps a little less rigid than Green, but not much. Every morning at five, his servant, Martin Lampe, a former soldier, would shake him awake roughly. Kant hated getting up early. So his day would begin. He'd drink a cup of weak tea, follow it with a bowl of tobacco, the preparations for his lectures, and writing until seven. He lectured in his home lecture theater from seven until eleven, after which he'd write some more until lunch, take a modest lunch at Zornig's coffee house on the Prinzessineplatz, preferring the company of ignorant soldiers to that of the many people who wanted to curry his favor or "hammer his head full" with their ideas and disputations. After lunch, he took a stroll and then visited Green. As he grew older, he still only smoked one pipe of tobacco a day, but the bowls of the pipes reputedly grew larger over time.

All inhabited landscapes, and some that are not, are constantly being read and translated in new editions. Kant's city, translated from German to Russian, has a complex beauty that you might not expect, certainly not if you read an article written in 2010 by Ben Judah for the UK journal *Standpoint*, in which Judah decries Kaliningrad as "one of the world's ugliest cities." Places change, but what Judah describes is a kind of stereotypical midnineties post-Soviet nightmare: "The factories have mostly closed. The jobs will not come back. Humiliated men without work turn to the bottle. Women talk about being abused. Their sons are not remotely equipped for the e-age."

The Kaliningrad I visit, three years after Judah's visit, is only in a vestigial sense like the city Judah disdains as "full of crumbling communist estates, with glinting neon hoardings. Maintenance is unheard of and faulty wiring hangs across dank, filthy socialist avenues, each wide enough for three tanks abreast." The crumbling communist estates, in any event, are not unique to Kaliningrad. Judah's new Russian Orthodox church in Victory Square is a "white slab of golden domes," the malls are empty, and with hardly anything bought. Women tart themselves up for sex tourists or advertise themselves as "your Russian bride." There is a pall of pollution in the air that tastes to him like toast.

No polluted mist hangs in the air now, no buttered toast smell. Young couples, not drunks, lounge on the benches near the cosmonaut statue. The electric lines that carry the current to the city's trams seem in good repair. To scan the boulevard across from Victory Square, full of men and women, some dressed fashionably, some not so, and imagine anything even vaguely "socialist" in the Soviet sense, or tanks three abreast, would require the dementia my mother suffered from when she imagined the Iraqi army unloading bodies on the pleasant avenues of the town in which she spent her dotage. Victory Square is alive with fountains. A toddler evades capture as his mother pursues him with his carriage. The Russian Orthodox church and its bell towers that dominate the square, along with a red obelisk, a memorial to the war, gleam indeed, but no more tastelessly than any gleaming dome.

In Jerusalem, an occasional pilgrim suffers from Jerusalem Syndrome, a psychotic break in which the sufferer believes they are Jesus or Mary or Joseph. Luckily for myself and Judah, neither of us think we are Kant. Kaliningrad is not Königsberg. It hasn't been for over seventy years. Those people are gone. That town is gone. In Judah's England, in the Rust Belt of the U.S., there are countless examples of cities in worse shape than Kaliningrad. But it's not what it once was, indisputably.

Königsberg Castle was dismantled by the Soviets after World War II, and in its spot erected a white building of Lego-like angles, known around Kaliningrad as "the Monster." You can go to town on the "What-was-then-known-as" game, and also the "On-this-spot-once-stood" game, in former Königsberg, then East Prussia, now Kaliningrad, Russia.

Following the path of Kant's daily walk today is mostly a depressing business with little that would have left him less than horrified. And you know you're in the right area because a neglected plaque along the way memorializes his famous quote, in German and in Russian: "Two things awe me most: the starry sky above and the moral law within me." If there's anything that produces awe here now, it's the fact of change itself—you won't find anything vaguely Kantian in the vicinity of his walk until you reach the reimagined faux historic buildings that make up Fish Village.

Two tram lines now intersect the spot where Kant once gave his lectures to packed audiences of students who sat in awe and terror. Many didn't understand him but wanted to say they had attended one of the great man's lectures. They lived in dread of his metaphysics and logic, but his lectures on anthropology were more entertaining. Now an electronic sign blinks dozens of advertisements a minute at the intersection, a lecture of economics, not reason.

THIRD MAXIM:
Better to Be a Fool in Fashion
Than a Fool Out of Fashion

Before the Black Hills were sacred to the Lakota Sioux, they lived in what's now known as Minnesota. Before a Jewish homeland was established in what's now known as Israel, other candidates for the homeland included Uganda and the western desert of Australia. Facts mean little when it comes to a people's attachment to the land, but the identity of a place is mutable, not a constant, though most of us want it to be so.

Before Kaliningrad became an exclave of Russia, it became an exclave of Germany. The Treaty of Versailles formally ending World War I ceded to Poland a large corridor to the Baltic that cut off East

Prussia, including Königsberg, from the rest of Germany. When Germany invaded Poland in 1939, the first troops landed on this corridor, conquered it, and for the next six years, Königsberg became an ex-exclave before changing its identity yet again.

In Kant's day, the Russians occupied Königsberg after Frederick the Great's troops were defeated at the Battle of Gross-Jägersdorf. Königsberg was ceded to Russia. For the next five years, Russian holidays were observed and Russian currency used. All public officials including university professors had to swear an oath to Empress Elizabeth. Kant had no problem with this. He didn't fawn over the Russians like Watson, the poetry instructor at the university, did. Neither did he keep his distance. He got along well enough with the Russians, especially as the Russians favored the university, and nothing much changed for the worse, only the better. The Russians acted more cultured than the Prussians, introducing French cuisine to the city. Königsberg had been a provincial town with ultraconservative mores, and the religious leaders frowned upon the scandalous things the Russians introduced: dinner parties, masked balls, and the drinking of punch. But Kant and his crowd felt liberated. The Russian officers liked to attend his lectures. Enacting a kind of social mobility he had never experienced before the Russians, he was often invited to fancy dinners at the homes of nobles, Russian officers, bankers, and merchants. Kant, a handsome man with blond hair, became a bit of a dandy during this part of his life, the color of his clothes following the color of the flowers in season, even wearing a ceremonial sword, though he never could have brandished one, due to his weak constitution, his hypochondriac nature. His guiding maxim of the time: better to be a fool in fashion than a fool out of fashion.

If the Russians had stayed forever that time, or at least the forever of Kant's lifetime, he may never have taken off that ceremonial sword and stopped the chitchat over punch. But the Russians eventually left and Kant stayed put. He had chances to leave as well, better opportunities at other universities than the ones afforded to him in Königsberg, but Königsberg defined him, and without his city, he felt lost. For quite a while, he had his eye on the professorship of logic and metaphysics at the university, and he waited for the position to open. When a professor of mathematics dropped dead, he sent a letter the next day to Berlin suggesting that Professor Buck, who held the position Kant wanted, should be moved to the vacated mathematics position and he should be installed as Professor of Logic and Metaphysics. After all, Professor Buck had obtained his position at the behest of the Russian government.

Fifteen days after he made his request, Kant was appointed to the position of Professor of Logic and Metaphysics. Buck was flummoxed. Why hadn't he even been consulted? Kant had said nothing to him. Buck had never once entertained a desire to be a professor of mathematics. But it hardly mattered. Kant didn't care what Buck wanted. Kant had pitted the wounded pride of the Prussians against the Russians with whom he, like Buck, had been on the friendliest of terms. Ever thus it was in the world of academe. It's fitting, then, that his grave was the sole survivor of the bombing of Kneiphof in 1945, and that the university that rose from the ashes of the one at which he taught moral law, now bears his name.

FOURTH MAXIM:
The Origin of Suffering Is Attachment

Within a few years of the end of World War II, few Germans remained in Königsberg: a dozen or so women who married Russians at the end of the war. The remaining Germans were deported by the Russians, the German POWs remaining only as long as they could help rebuild Kaliningrad. The region or oblast of Kaliningrad became for the Soviets, terra nullius, a place devoid of people needing to be resettled with Soviet pioneers.

In Kant's view of the perfect world, visitors were always welcome, but they weren't supposed to stay. They were supposed to treat their hosts well, unlike those people of "civilized" nations who, by way of visiting other lands, conquered them, considered them "lands without owners, for they counted the inhabitants as nothing." But the situation after World War II wasn't as clear-cut as white settlers displacing Native Americans in North America or Aboriginals in Australia. The Prussians themselves hadn't been exemplars of good manners on their four-year-long sojourn in Russia.

The Soviets' propaganda campaign promised the new Russian settlers land, a cow, and a German house. Most of the thousands who flocked to the Oblast received none of this, but by then this blasted land was their new home, with no return from where they'd come. The strong feeling persisted among the settlers that this was *not* their home, their uncertainty evident in the postwar architecture of Kaliningrad, in what's absent. In Kaliningrad, Brezhnev- and Khrushchev-era apartment blocks dominate, but there is little in the way of Stalinist architecture. For the first twenty years or so, life in Kaliningrad felt temporary. Whatever German structure seemed salvageable was restored, and not simply out of frugality but also from timidity. Any month, any week, any day, the rightful owners might come knocking.

They didn't. They couldn't. The Soviets installed in Kaliningrad a huge military installation of one hundred thousand men. Two thirds of the Soviet Baltic Fleet was stationed there. For all outsiders, including those who had been born in one-time Königsberg, especially them, the Oblast was off limits.

A Russian joke: An adventurous young tapeworm emerges from someone's ass so that he can explore the world. He travels the world and sees snowcapped mountains, jungles, the great oceans, birds flying through the sky. Upon his return, he reenters the rectum where he was born, and he immediately asks his mother, "Why do we have to live in all this shit, Mom?" His mother answers, "Just stay put, Son, this is your motherland."

Kaliningrad was indeed a version of the shithole that Ben Judah describes. Certainly this was the case after the war that destroyed it, but people, unlike tapeworms, are sometimes able to transform where they live into something better than a shithole, even if what the place once was is forever out of reach. For authenticity's sake and the tourist ruble, people try all the same, hence the Epcot Centers of the world, the Williamsburgs, the small "Fish Village" (across from the supermarket, sex shop, and Brezhnevian apartment block sentinels) of Kaliningrad along the Pregolya River, with its wan imitations of eighteenth- and nineteenth-century cafés.

Here, no place is simply itself, and that's what lends Kaliningrad its complexity, making it one of the sad, beautiful places of the world. Every building is a combination of what it was once and what it is now; the people of Kaliningrad can never forget this completely, not that they want to forget. The complexity of a city such as this transcends the usual tourist experience.

FIFTH MAXIM:
No Matter What the Holiday, Celebrate It!
(And Ignore the Contradictions)

Russian Federation Day is in full swing at the Central Park of Culture and Leisure, formerly Luisenwahl Park, by midafternoon. Instituted by Boris Yeltsin in the 1990s for a newly created country, the Russian Federation, the holiday is not marked by the fervent strain of nationalism you might find on May Day, or Victory Day, or even Victory over Japan Day. Russian Federation Day! Such a banal and unthreatening ring it has—though a pleasant sort of banality, more the sort of thing you'd find in America as a greeting card company's ploy. National Secretaries Day, or some kind of civic-minded festival like Taste of Poughkeepsie.

"Happy Russia Day!" a banner proclaims at the entrance to the park, amid a mattress of red, white, and blue balloons. The flag on the banner isn't exactly the simple red white and blue stripes of the Russian flag, but a somewhat nostalgic, if not conflicted, hearkening back to history, displaying both the Russian eagles of the old monarchy and an emblem of St. George slaying the dragon. There is not an actual Russian flag in sight, which seems charming and a little odd.

Amid the leafy grounds of the park, stalls line the paths, vendors hawk cheap earrings, weavers weave, babushkas on green park benches watch the action, children are led by on ponies, and people sell food: kebabs called *shaslik* and a pilaf-like dish called *plov*. There is no beer tent, alas, though you can probably score a cold cup of Kvas, the mildly fermented drink popular throughout Russia.

For now, a red-bearded man in his thirties, wearing a traditional cassock and a microphone, teaches a group of bystanders Russian square dances, belting out instructions and berating a boy for being too shy with his partner. Carnival rides swirl in one quadrant of the park and people take photos while sitting in the lap of a brooding statue in the enormous likeness of Vladimir Vysotsky, a national music icon the likes of Bob Dylan or John Lennon. Three folklore choirs, made up largely of children and young adults, serenade one another with traditional Russian songs, while nearby men dressed as Teutonic knights engage in sword play.

Hold on. Teutonic knights? At the park's large bandstand in the park, a group of Ukrainian men and women dance and sing. Isn't that sort of like having Canadians at a Fourth of July celebration? They're followed by a belly dancer gyrating to Arabic music while smoke billows around her. A troupe of eleven young women from Armenia, long braids draped over their flowing white robes, dance to balalaikas and autoharps. A Belorussian group of five stout women play the accordion and belt out folksy music. Does this celebration feel less Russian than Soviet, the move of an empire displaying the diverse cultural riches of its farthest reaches? That's one way of reading it. You can also read this as a simple display of cultural diversity—though when was cultural diversity ever simple?

Stalin liked moving people around, to put it mildly. For the Jews, he fabricated an ersatz homeland in Siberia called Birobidzhan. Koreans he moved to Kazakhstan. Even ethnic Germans he put in their place, though not the place they wanted. Stalin deported them by the thousands to the Volga region and Kazakhstan during the war. When the Soviet Union collapsed, several thousand of these ethnic Germans and their progeny moved to the Kaliningrad Oblast "as a compromise," according to Evgeny Vinokurov, an economist and one of the world's leading experts on enclaves and exclaves. They wanted to be close to relatives in both Germany and Russia. A somewhat odd choice of a place to settle, such an unsettled place of liminal identity, especially, you'd think, for a German. But perhaps they're the perfect settlers precisely because of that mixed identity.

At a stand selling homemade dolls in ethnic garb, the only dolls left to purchase are those representing the former Soviet republics. All the purely Russian dolls have been snatched up, the closest sentiment of Russian nationalism in view all day.

SIXTH MAXIM:

You Can Be Loyal to an Institution, but Don't
Expect the Institution to Be Loyal to You

In Moscow, ten thousand protestors have gathered today for the "March against Executioners," but here in Kaliningrad, those who do not see this as a day of celebration, but as a day of outrage and rebellion, have only mustered a dozen participants. They've chosen one of the main theaters of patriotism for their protest, a central plaza of Kaliningrad, beneath a Soviet-era statue of Mother Russia bearing the grief of her war dead with grim pride—a symbol of another era. The protestors hold their signs dutifully, but not as grimly as Mother Russia, some milling about as if at a cocktail party, chatting and laughing, both protestors and an equal number of bored police in silent agreement, it seems. Perhaps the protestors actually outnumber the police if you count the baby in its carriage, beside its banner-wielding mother.

One of the protestors, a skinny woman in her thirties named Anna, says there have been more protestors in the past. The message on their banners are fighting words: "Oligarchy is the mother of disorder," "In battle is where you acquire your rights," "Hierarchal power demands victims." But there's no fighting in Kaliningrad—not now, not today at least. In the Central Park of Culture and Leisure, Spiderman has cajoled a young boy to pose for a photo. In the Skipper Hotel in Fish Village, a young hotel clerk chats with the restaurant manager about his recent trip to Berlin while the Red Army Chorus belts out patriotic songs on the lobby TV. In the Kaliningrad Zoo, a woman in her forties and her teenage daughter explore the slabs jutting from the earth with Kant's words on them, the mother's eyes slipping over the text before hurrying on to the lion exhibit, the thing they came to see. Her shoes are too tight and she wants an ice cream cone and a cigarette, but besides that, she feels content to spend this holiday with her daughter, whose pretty face has been marred too often by sullenness lately. Maybe after the zoo, she'll treat her daughter to a meal at McDonalds. That's always been something they've bonded over: their shared love of fries.

SEVENTH MAXIM:
Those Who Cross the Sea, Change
the Sky, but Nor Their Souls

Evgeny Vinokurov grew up in a formerly German house in Kaliningrad that lay in ruin until 1957. Both of his grandfathers fought in the war and in 1946 ended up in Austria where they met their future wives, one a nurse, the other a supply office worker. Today, he favors changing the city's name back to Königsberg, though that name isn't the only option. It could be renamed something like Baltisk. But the majority of Kaliningraders don't agree with him, nor does Moscow, made nervous by any change that harkens back to what the city once was. Any country's main directive is to maintain its sovereignty, the foundation of patriotism and nationalism. If you can name a place, you can lay a claim to it, hence China's current foreign policy claiming virtually all of the South China Sea. Place names can cause wars and often do. In the early 2000s, populist national candidates often played the Kaliningrad card, issuing dire warnings that the Oblast wanted to break away to become part of Germany, Lithuania, or even Sweden.

That's about as likely as the city being renamed Putingrad. Sociologists have been taking polls for over a decade and have found Kaliningraders' sense of identity fairly stable. Only 2 percent say they want to be part of Germany and another 5 percent want to form a fourth Baltic republic. At least as many Alaskans and Hawaiians would leave the U.S. if they had the chance. Probably twice as many Texans and Californians.

Kaliningrad is Russian because Russians live there. If Kaliningrad had mostly Germans living in it, then the Kremlin would have reason to worry. The difference is akin to that between the Falklands and Hong Kong. The Falkland Island inhabitants are largely Brits, not Argentines, and so they have no desire to be Argentinian. But Hong Kong is largely Chinese, and while the identity of the Hong Kong Chinese is always an issue and consequently fragile, threatened by their sense of political difference from Beijing, they nonetheless do not wish to be British. Few tears were shed by the Chinese citizens of Hong Kong when the British lowered the Union Jack for the last time in 1997.

From an economic view, it would be useful for Kaliningrad if EU members could visit the Oblast visa-free, in Vinokurov's view.

The local Duma lobbied Moscow on that point twice, and both times the proposals were rejected "quite rudely." Emissaries from Moscow were dispatched to Kaliningrad with the message, "No, this will never happen."

Everyone except Moscow seems to understand that the page has turned irrevocably for Königsberg. Even the old guard Prussians have given up. In 1990, the Homeland Association of East Prussia counted a hundred thousand members—an influential conservative force in German politics, but no more. The East Prussians of old have mostly died off, and their children and grandchildren have largely ceased to care. Or perhaps the yearning has simply been subsumed by other day-to-day considerations and will manifest itself again in a thousand years.

In the meantime, the nostalgia from the old Germans who visited Kaliningrad and wept in the nineties has, like their zoo, been inherited by Kaliningraders, partially a commercial nostalgia but not entirely. Photos of German street scenes from the turn of the twentieth century abound in restaurants and offices around the city, and the city takes pride in the old German castles, ruins, and nineteenth-century fortifications outside of the city proper. In Kraków, Poland, a group of Roman Catholics started a Jewish Festival, the world's largest, running strong now in its third decade, because they wanted to know who these Jews were who had made up half their population before the war. Should it be any different for Russians living in a formerly German city?

As a university student in 1998, Evgeny Vinokurov studied German at the University of Marburg, and there he met a retired professor of religious history born in the East Prussia town of Trakehnen in 1926. Wounded in the war in April 1945, the man was transported from the front on a hospital ship to West Germany afterwards.

Despite the age difference, and the clash of their personal histories and places of birth, they got along well and Evgeny invited the man to visit him in Kaliningrad, which he did the following summer, taking the train from Berlin and spending ten days with Evgeny's family. The city was uglier than it is today, but the old man seemed unfazed, saying that he well understood this was Russia now, not Germany.

Trakehnen had been renowned for the powerful horses that were bred there from the early 1700s at the behest of Frederick the First of Prussia. Kant would have admired such horses, famous in his day as war horses, a favorite of the Russian Imperial Army. Perhaps some of the Russian officers who listened to Kant's lectures bought their horses from Trakehnen. And he would have seen them working in the fields when he took his occasional carriage rides in the country with Joseph Green.

Between the world wars, Trakehners became the most famous sports breed in the world, but by the end of World War II, only a few hundred of the horses survived, led on a legendary trek by some brave souls across a partly frozen sea to escape to the West. Along the way, the Russian air force further thinned the ranks of the fleeing Prussians and their horses by shredding the ice with their machine guns during the day, scores of horses and people drowning in the churning sea. The kind of sport young men perverted by war can only play at such times. And the town from which they fled, the "City of Horses," fared no better, laid waste and renamed ironically by the Russians, Yasnaya Polyana, the name of Tolstoy's estate.

The religious history professor from Marburg, wounded and evacuated, had not been back since. The drive to Yasnaya Polyana took several hours, and by the time Evgeny and his family arrived, the normally chatty professor received the vision of this shattered place in silence: the horse farms gone, the drunks falling down in the streets of the ruined village, the streets leading to the shattered school he had once attended. For the rest of the return trip, the entire three hours, he was silent, except for muttering one word that Evgeny, sharing in his friend's disappointment, heard. After that trip, predictably, they lost touch.

If anything of old Prussia survives, you can see it most authentically in the dressage event at the Olympics: Trakehner horses prancing and strutting, their elegant bearing, their name intact.

EIGHTH MAXIM:
We're All World Citizens in the Boneyard

It's delusional to think that land, indifferent nature, could yearn for a people the way a people yearn for the land. And yet, there's a case for just that, even if it's a kind of collective delusion. Visit some of the other sad, beautiful places of the world, where a people have been decimated or displaced, Tasmania or the Cathar country of Southern France, which once held populations of Aboriginals and Albigensians, respectively, and try to see the land as similar to any other land. Even if you didn't know the land's history . . . but let's stop there. It's ridiculous. You *do* know it's history and that's the point. And so you can't help but think that the land's emptied castles, its very hills and streams, yearn for someone else. Perhaps it would have been better if you'd never read Chief Seattle's famous speech:

> Every part of this soil is sacred in the estimation of my people. Every hillside, every valley, every plain and grove, has been hallowed by some sad or happy event in days long vanished. Even the rocks, which seem to be dumb and dead as they swelter in the sun along the silent shore, thrill with memories of stirring events connected with the lives of my people, and the very dust upon which you now stand responds more lovingly to their footsteps than yours, because it is rich with the blood of our ancestors, and our bare feet are conscious of the sympathetic touch. . . . And when the last Red Man shall have perished, and the memory of my tribe shall have

become a myth among the White Men, these shores will swarm with the invisible dead of my tribe, and when your children's children think themselves alone in the field, the store, the shop, upon the highway, or in the silence of the pathless woods, they will not be alone. In all the earth there is no place dedicated to solitude. At night when the streets of your cities and villages are silent and you think them deserted, they will throng with the returning hosts that once filled them and still love this beautiful land.

On the day Kant died in 1804, the frozen earth of Königsberg didn't want to accept him, but since then Kant could not be moved from Königsberg, not even in death. Not even bombs could dislodge him. The stars have not changed much in the sky and the moral law hasn't changed much, either, but everything else from the walk he took each day to the name of the city in which he spent his life, and its people, have changed. What, then, is this piece of land? Is it really any more Kaliningrad than it is Königsberg? What makes it any place at all and its people any people? Who belongs here? The only person indisputably who seems to belong here is Kant.

Perhaps Kant was simply a more dramatic example of the way most human beings feel about their homes—that their homes define them—when, really, it's the other way around. Kant and Chief Seattle aside, all our homes were something else once before and will be something entirely different in the future. Kant never had to confront this problem in his lifetime, as did the Prussian professor of religious history from Trakehnen. The professor must have understood finally on the silent journey home from Trakehnen that his sense of belonging to a land had simply been a collective but necessary delusion: the thing that made him Prussian. Necessary because without this delusion there's nothing except for the perilous passage across the nearly frozen seas through which we trek in our own solitudes. And what is laid waste is what we lead forward invisibly, the collective herd, our fragile inheritances.

So let's not forget it's Russian Federation Day, a day of recalibration, if not celebration. Little in the Central Park of Culture and Leisure recalls Prussia, though this ground has been hallowed by sad and happy events, and soaked with Prussian blood. It's true, there are no places on earth dedicated to solitude, not even Antarctica— one tribe or another has experienced them all and, when possible, claimed them. Today, any lingering Prussian ghosts might feel especially forlorn. If Kant's ghost sits on a bench among the babushkas, he must be waiting for nightfall, when the last of the fireworks have tailed away, the park has emptied of cultural and leisurely Russians and, looking up, he might still hope to detect immutable laws.

Field Notes for the
Graveyard Enthusiast

In creating a taxonomy of graveyards, let's start with the obvious:
Graveyards in Which We Are Not Buried along with Graveyards
in Which We Are Buried. At first glance, both of these classifica-
tions would seem simple enough. The first consists of all graveyards Known and Unknown, and the second contains no graveyards,
Known or Unknown. Given a few years, our relationship to these
categories might well change. The first category will contain all but
one graveyard, and the second will contain that same graveyard,
while excluding all the rest. If, however, you choose cremation,
the categories will remain unaltered from your first encounter with
them. As a Jew, more superstitious than observant, cremation is not
an option for me—I can't, in any case, separate this option from the
fate of so many of my coreligionists at the hands of the Nazis. As
I age, the consideration of where to be buried occupies more and
more of my time, in direct contrast to the fading of my preoccupa-
tion with where to live. My father and sister are buried in a rural
cemetery in Athens, Ohio, while my mother, grandmother, and several other relatives are buried in a vast necropolis in Queens, New
York. Considering this split in my family, which bears absolutely no
relation to their closeness in life (my father and sister were often at
odds, while my mother was extraordinarily devoted to them both),
I feel an almost giddy amount of latitude in my eventual choice—
happily, I have always loved graveyards, but my enthusiasm for so
many graveyards makes me unable to settle on one, to settle down,

as it were. As I am a restless spirit in life, unable to choose a more or less permanent place to live, never having lived in one place for more than nine years in my half a century on earth, I imagine I will make an equally restive spirit. If I had the means, I might simply have a codicil in my will drawn up, obligating my heirs to disinter me every few years and move my remains to some new pleasant or unusual location. As this eccentric request is unlikely to be followed, even if I somehow accrue the riches necessary to make the request financially possible, I suppose I must choose one. I'll leave that decision for another day and instead will spend these several hours of my existence contemplating some of the varieties of graveyards, trying to convey some measure of my enthusiasm for them.

As a child, I used to hold my breath when passing a graveyard, but now I breathe deeply—in any event, there will be plenty of time for holding my breath. If you are a breath holder, imagining holding your breath does some good, then you might want to forego this small tour of graveyards I Have Known and Loved, and instead eat some ice cream or have a tumble in bed, both activities I would take to the grave if I could.

Perhaps the two largest categories of graveyards are Graveyards Known and Graveyards Unknown. A subset of the latter is Graveyards Forgotten and a subset of the former is Graveyards of Historic Note. A subset of either category is Unintended Graveyards or Cemeteries of Happenstance. These would include mass graves, or as yet undiscovered graveyards. Of the latter, we might surmise that graves are all around us, from the unmarked graves of vanquished, if not forgotten, peoples, to some spot in the woods where a lone traveler froze in the snow, starved, or sat down feeling ill by a tree and never stood again. Under the streets of London, for instance, lie at least thirty-seven thousand bodies, according to the *London Times*. Is it proper to call the city of London a graveyard? Perhaps in the strict sense, no, but conceptually, let's consider the graveyard's boundaries as limitless as the earth's, at least potentially so. In this way, we begin to demystify the graveyard (and possibly death) while conversely making into sacred, if not consecrated, space every inch on which we tread.

Walking through a graveyard is how most of us, at least those not in the medical profession or undertakers, come into our closest contact with death while remaining alive. An appreciation of this vast category of Unknown Graveyards is the cornerstone for a kind of mindfulness that those who don't hold their breath have when walking through a Known Graveyard—we might, as the Japanese do, hold a picnic by the grave of a relative, share beer and rice crackers, and enjoy our outing while at the same time including our loved ones. Whether or not I might enjoy Spirit beer and crackers, I like the thought of at least being included. When Janis Joplin treated her friends to a round of drinks in the afterlife, she had the right idea, but perhaps she shouldn't have stopped there. Perhaps she might have requested to be entombed beneath her favorite bar, not that she might continue to let the good times roll, but so the combination of spirits and Spirit might give patrons a buzz that was simultaneously intoxicating and sobering. It's this paradoxical and powerful combination of inebriation and sobriety that is one of my aims as a devotee of the Unknown Graveyard.

The antithesis of the Unknown Graveyard is the Graveyard of Historic Note. Of these, the largest subset by far is the Military Graveyard. I'm stopped (dead, I'd like to say) in my tracks, left speechless at most such graveyards. Most recently, I visited the town of Aquileia in Northern Italy, a town within a region that has changed hands and nationalities innumerable times, once the second biggest town in the Roman Empire. My companion wanted to visit the ancient mosaics that line the subfloor of the basilica that was later built on top of the Roman temple. I'm not the biggest fan of either mosaics or basilicas—perhaps having seen so many splendid cathedrals over the years that they have blurred. As for mosaics, well, after exclaiming how meticulous the craftsmanship is, I quickly become bored by shallow Roman faces staring up at me, or birds or lions. No matter how beautiful the image, virtually none of them will stay with me longer than five minutes after viewing, unless I take a photo. I've ceased carrying a camera while traveling because I never look at trip photos and no one else is interested.

Attached to this church was a graveyard, and for me the graveyard was a hundred times more fascinating than the Roman mosaics. This was a cemetery of the fallen: Cimitero dei Caduti of World War I. In this shaded courtyard lay perhaps a hundred soldiers whose deaths were as strikingly meaningless as any I've ever heard of. This was a Hapsburg Cemetery—the men buried here died fighting to prop up the Austro-Hungarian Empire that collapsed as a result of this war. The cemetery is replete with iron crosses and encased photographs, dating to World War I, of young and middle-aged mustachioed men with stiff hats and stiff expressions that have somehow withstood the elements.

"Mario Brva," reads one inscription. "*Mori per la Patria.*" But what country did he die for? As his name and the names of others suggest, part of his name was Italian and part Slovenian. In this region of the Istrian Peninsula, Hapsburg census takers were often confounded by the question of ethnicity. A village might self-identify one year as Italian and ten years later as Slovenian, depending on what the parish priest told them to say they were. Almost a hundred years after these men died in a war fighting for a monarchy that no longer existed, I was left feeling more bereaved than if I had been standing in front of the thousands of white crosses at Normandy. At Normandy, at least, I could make sense of why the men had died in such vast numbers, but not in Aquileia. Citizens of Austro-Hungary, perhaps they would have preferred to give their lives for Italy. Or perhaps they would have preferred to die for Slovenia. Perhaps they would have been happy not to die for any country whose existence was as fragile as their own.

To offset these ironies, I suppose, the people who had designed this graveyard aimed for greater glory by commissioning a statue of Christ supporting two fallen soldiers. The statue, a massive chunk of marbled sentiment, depicts Christ on the cross, or mostly on the cross. He has freed his right hand from its nail and reaches down to touch the brow of a dying soldier, the soldier's face lifted like a beseeching child to the savior's face, a model of compassion and pity. Below the dying man lies another soldier, already dead, but the dying man has a hold on his dead comrade, lifting him up, too, to heaven. All three men are bare-chested, though Christ, at least, doesn't wear a cartridge belt like the other two. The statue, of course, is largely ignored by the few other tourists in this courtyard. On the day I visited, I, alone, succumbed to the great sentimentality of this statue, feeling pity for everyone involved, including the donors and the sculptor.

Often, though not always, the Military Graveyard, the Historic Graveyard, as well as what we might term the Cemetery of Happenstance, are linked, but not always (as in the case of London—a Cemetery of Happenstance, but neither military, nor particularly historic, as a graveyard). A famous example of the Military-Historic-Happenstance Graveyard is the Little Bighorn Battlefield, which was never intended (by Custer at least) as a graveyard. The soldiers in Custer's detail were buried in the spots at which they fell—220 bodies were later reinterred in a single spot on Last Stand Hill, except for Custer's body, which was transferred to a grave at West Point, and a number of the officers under his command, which were shipped back to Eastern cemeteries. But the markers remain in the spots where the soldiers fell, and in recent years new markers have been added in locations where Cheyenne and Sioux warriors reportedly perished. And so, the remarkable feature of this graveyard is that, unlike any other Known Graveyards (at least by me), one can mark the progress of a battle by the location of the points of death. There's something immediate and visceral about seeing a battle marked in such a way. Instead of the ordered and stately crosses of Normandy and Arlington, perhaps it would be wiser in the long run to bury all casualties in all wars on the spots where they died. Imagine coming upon such reminders at random in some European village or city—we should see death inflicted by war, in any event, as surprising, random, chaotic, not ordered and stately.

In some cases, an Unknown-Happenstance-Military Graveyard (belonging, as in the cases of all Military Graveyards Known and Unknown, to the larger category: Graveyards in Which I Am Not Buried) will shift categories to Known-Happenstance-Military-Historic Graveyard. One such instance, on which I'd like to touch briefly, is the Japanese Military Graveyard on the island of Corregidor in the Philippines. On this island, General Douglas MacArthur's American and Filipino forces held at bay the Japanese Imperial forces from December 1941 until May 1942, far longer than the superior Japanese forces anticipated. When MacArthur and President Quezon of the Philippines were smuggled off the island before the island fell to the Japanese, he made his famous "I shall return" declaration. Like MacArthur, I have had a repeated urge to return to Corregidor, too, though for different reasons. If one believes in ghosts, then this island is surely haunted. The entire island is, in essence, a graveyard. Not an inch was spared by Japanese guns in taking it at the beginning of the war, nor an inch spared by American guns reclaiming it. Ruined bunkers, hulks of gigantic guns, barracks with trees and metal cables and twisted vines grown together, even the ruins of a movie theater, dot the island. Here is where the memorial to the War in the Pacific was placed, but this memorial has about as much relevance to war as a bombardier's eye to his target. The real memorials are the ruins and the graves—here, the Japanese graveyard holds the most promise for the graveyard enthusiast because it is the rarest of military graveyards. For many years, its location was unknown, but was rediscovered forty years after the war. Very well-tended now, the memorial has a spectacular view and a large statue of the Goddess of Mercy, upon whose foot my Filipino guide, a man old enough to have been a child during the war, made a point of taking a piss on when we stopped at this site.

Graves We Might Piss On could take up pages of notes, perhaps starting with Hitler's unmarked grave in a parking lot of the former East Berlin and no doubt including the well-marked grave of Custer at West Point. But let's not go there, to coin a phrase, or else we might veer off onto a bitter tangent that strays too far from our aim, which is, after all, to familiarize ourselves with our eventual homes rather than alienate ourselves further.

Instead, we might consider Historic Graveyards that are not Military Cemeteries. These include your standards: Père Lachaise and the Pantheon in Paris, the catacombs of Rome, as well as Recoleta in Buenos Aires. We might also include most such cemeteries in a subcategory of Historic Graveyards: Known Graveyards in Which Famous People Are Buried. We must acknowledge at the same time that not all Famous People are Buried in Historic Graveyards, nor are all graveyards necessarily considered Historic if, say, one famous person is buried there, or if that person's star fades over time; not all the graves of famous people are Known. But of Known Graveyards in Which Famous People are Buried, few hold my attention or interest for long. I have little interest in visiting Molière or Jim Morrison at Père Lachaise, nor Victor Hugo and Marie Curie at the Pantheon. At Recoleta, I was more interested in the graveyard's cats than in the tomb of Evita. And I would surely skip the Catacombs of Callixtus in which assorted popes and martyrs are entombed in favor of the anonymous stacks of skulls in the Capuchin Crypt, or in favor of the so-called Bone Church of Kutna Hora in the Czech

Republic in which the bleached skulls and bones of forty thousand victims of the fifteenth-century Hussite Wars and Black Plague were arranged in the church in 1878 into chandeliers, crowns, chalices, and bells made of bones and skulls. While studying a blackbird made of bones pecking out the eye of a Turk (the Schwartzenberg family coat of arms, the family that commissioned this ossuary), I marvel at the thought that the skull of the Turk was never a Turk at all in real life, but some poor local peasant struck down by illness, that in death he or she has achieved a kind of anonymous fame. The fact of the skull reminds me of the fact that he was a person once with a life, a history, passions, and unhappiness—someone whose sense of personhood has been as bleached as thoroughly as his bones.

For this reason and others, the Famous hold much less interest to me in death than the Anonymous dead. While viewing the crypts at Westminster, for instance, my thoughts of death are subsumed by thoughts of fame. The anonymous dead are my brethren, and to the skulls of Kutna Hora, I can imagine adding my own to the fragile pile, from which nothing tumbles. At Pompeii, I can gaze for an hour as at a painting by a master at the anonymous pyroclastic cast of a slave forever trying to shield his face from the mountain that has buried him.

Perhaps the largest category of Graveyard, in any case, is Graveyards in Which the Anonymous Lie, a grouping that contains nearly every graveyard, Known and Unknown. My favorite of these—and I use the word "favorite" advisedly—is Auschwitz. People are buried in the form of ash at various points in the death camp, but these are not the most affecting gravesites—still, the various urns made out of ash are perhaps the closest we Jews have to reliquaries. Each room at Auschwitz is a tomb of sorts, each containing, if not actual DNA of the departed, then something of their history and humanity. We follow our guide to the room of women's shoes, to the room of prayer shawls, to the room of artificial limbs and crutches, to the room of eyeglasses, to the room of pots and pans, to the room of suitcases and baskets, to the display of broken dolls. The suitcases are grave markers as are all the other markers. On many of the suitcases are stamped the names and sometimes the date of birth and the city from which they came.

Klement Hedwig
8 10 1898

Jnes Meyer
Koln

Neumann Friedrich
1890

My own aunt Rose was one of the 430,000 Hungarian Jews brought here toward the end of the war. My father's family were all Hungarian Jews. Those who didn't emigrate surely perished here or in nearby Birkenau.

This is the closest I can come to visiting their graves. At Auschwitz there is a room of hair, two tons of it. Every prisoner was shaved, and the hair that was of any length was sold for half a mark per kilo. The two tons of hair behind the window in the room of hair at Auschwitz represents forty thousand people, only a fraction of the seven tons of hair the Soviets found here, which itself was only a fraction of the hair that was shorn from the prisoners about to meet their deaths. The hair has all turned gray over time because of the light, but once it contained all the colors that hair can be; and here, as close as anywhere you can stand, you stare at stacks of bodies disguised as filaments.

Perhaps I should include Auschwitz in the category Graveyards in Which I Am Buried, a category I previously thought uninhabited. At first glance, this might seem merely a sentimental gesture, or grandly symbolic, but I would argue that all graves are sentimental gestures, all of them grandly symbolic. That makes them no less necessary, but does one really take up residence in the ground? As with an honorary degree, an honorary burial has little in the way of actual benefit, and so I must include myself in Auschwitz in the honorary sense—my connection to the place, in any case, is not arbitrary.

But here I'd like to add a tiny category of graveyard that the enthusiast should not miss or fail to notice: the Graveyard Guarded by Avatars. Before now, I have tried to keep my feet on the ground, as it were, considering that my subject itself is so earthbound. Yet graveyards exist as habitats for living things as well as dead; and while the animals that inhabit these spaces might do so solely out of a need for unoccupied space, certain species take on the form almost of sentinels at the graveyards they occupy. The cats of Recoleta cemetery in Buenos Aires, for instance, seem like perfect companions for the wealthy inhabitants of the grand mausoleums that crowd the streets of the cemetery. From around corners, they peer at you, as if to question your intentions and to report your business. At Auschwitz, I noticed only pigeon caretakers, unconcerned, as pigeons almost always are, by the proximity of people, except when these visitors chase them or otherwise seem a potential threat.

The day after Auschwitz, I visited the Jewish Cemetery in Kraków. This cemetery belongs to the subset of Historic Graveyard that might be termed Graveyards of Lost Civilizations. The "New Jewish Cemetery" ("new" only in the sense that it is distinguishable from the nearby Medieval Jewish cemetery) holds many more dead Jews than the city of Kraków holds live ones. While the Jewish population of Kraków numbered a quarter of the city's inhabitants, or about 60,000, at the outbreak of WWII, only about 150 self-identified Jews remain in the city. The day I found the cemetery, I was the only live Jew (or live human of any kind) inside the graveyard. It was me and a minyan of pigeons milling around as I walked among the ancient trees and ancient gravestones, many graves well-tended still, and stretching the length and width of a sports arena to its far walls. As I always do in graveyards, I read the gravestones and tried to imagine what the lives of these people might have been. I came across relatively new gravestones as well as older:

Mauryey Wiener
ADWOKAT
1906–1990

Helena Goldman
1909–1983

Helena Krischer
1902, Krakov-
Bergen Belsen, 1945

A number of the graves had stones on them, a sign of remembrance that's part of Jewish tradition. I gathered up a dozen stones, then another dozen, and placed them on the graves with the most faded inscriptions, many completely illegible. I placed stone on stone—a stone finally is the only price the dead expect, the only language worth sharing. For the graveyard enthusiast, it's best to always have a pocketful.

Jews say Kaddish for the dead and remember the day of death, the Yahrzeit. Remembering feels good but forgetting is inevitable. In the graveyard we all lie down together, the Remembered and the Merely Dead. It's not with acrimony that I say the Remembered will also eventually be merely dead, but to point out that the solace of anonymity is what bonds us finally with every other human. My gravestone will be blank. In that way, I will have beat Time to the punch. This wish, at least, I expect my heirs to carry out.

Survivor Stories

As with most events in the Philippines, this one will start late. It's the mayor's birthday today, and the mayor doesn't want Manila to forget this, so he has scheduled a massive celebration and fireworks display by the waterfront. Unable to run again for office, he will do the next best thing and offer up his politically inexperienced son on this day to run in his stead. Traffic, which on the best of days in Manila is hopelessly snarled, is today beyond hopeless—abjectly snarled, let's say, because of the mayor's desire for us to remember his birthday and his cherished son.

I've come often to the Adriatico Arms Hotel in the tattered tourist district of Malate over the years—I suppose you might call it a boutique hotel with its air of tired elegance. I've sometimes sat here in this dining room and wondered what it would have been like to be in this spot at the end of World War II when the Japanese defenders of the city, facing certain defeat from General MacArthur's forces, went on a rampage and in the span of a single month systematically exterminated tens of thousands of innocent Filipinos. One hundred thousand Filipinos died in that last month, an average of over three thousand a day, some from American shells, but most at the hands of the Japanese. I've often wondered about this time and place, because that's what I do, I suppose, out of curiosity and habit. I wander and wonder, projecting myself back and forth in time and imagination, and thinking about being in another's shoes. As an exchange student in Osaka, Japan, in the 1970s, I read Jun'ichirō

Tanizaki's classic *Makioka Sisters*, set in the days before World War II, and I also wondered what it would have been like to be in that city during the war. Of course, such wandering would have been impossible. In Osaka, I would have been imprisoned, maybe shot, starved, beaten. In Manila, I would have been beheaded as countless civilians were during those last days.

This spot where the hotel now stands was in the thick of it. One day, in the last throes of the war, a woman sent her children off to play at a friend's house—when they returned, she was gone, taken by the Japanese and murdered, right next door to where we have gathered tonight.

There are places in the world where the same would happen to me now. As an American Jew, there are places where I might be taken and beheaded, even in the south of the Philippines, on the island where my wife was born. A week ago, we were there visiting her mother in Kidapawan, Mindanao—security was tight because of a summit of the ASEAN countries on the nearby island of Cebu to arrive at a joint policy on terrorism. Two days after my visit, a spot where I had stood was bombed, and three people were injured. In another nearby town, a bomb exploded at the same time and several died.

But tonight, I'm safe, I suppose, as safe as I can ever be in the world. Tonight we have gathered to watch a film by my friend Peter Parsons, not quite twenty years my senior. Peter is a ropy, athletic man whose father, Chick Parsons, was a war hero, one of MacArthur's most trusted commanders who organized the guerilla fighters against the Japanese in the Philippines and was at the top of the Japanese most-wanted list. Peter's father managed to smuggle himself and his family out of the country on a Panamanian consular passport, then returned to wreak havoc among the Japanese. I first met Peter and his brothers in 1999 while I was researching my book on the Tasaday and he was working on a documentary about his father.

As with much of history, this particular splinter of it is misunderstood and barely remembered. To Peter, the Japanese atrocities in Manila at the end of the war are on a par with the more famous atrocities in Nanking, brought to light by Iris Chang's *The Rape of Nanking*. Why, I wonder, as I sit at the table waiting for the invited guests to filter in, must we remember? The easy answer, the bromide, the George Santayana reason, is so that history won't repeat itself. But that's hopeless. History continually repeats itself, no matter how much we remember; and the world, by and large, is against remembering, encourages forgetting, in fact. I can't presume to know why exactly Iris Chang killed herself, but I'm sure that remembering in the face of the world's desire to continue on its merry way couldn't have helped. In order to live, to function, to enjoy, we must put aside the suffering of others.

"Fucking Manila," one of the guests mutters as he calls one of the other invited guests on his cell phone. Various people who've made it here through the mayor's traffic jam are calling up people who are still absent. The story is the same—Manila is at a standstill.

But slowly, the dining room fills. The room has an almost Spanish feel to it: wrought iron tables with marble tops, a tile floor, and a small bar behind which the waitstaff stand in attitudes both friendly and distant. They are the only people in the room who don't mingle except to bring out food—them and me. I'm not good at mingling. I never have been. I stand amid the twenty guests as though I've come to a fork in a path and can't decide which way to go. I hold a beer in my hand and stare at the condensation while listening to these people, many of whom have known one another for sixty years. The youngest is a boy in his early twenties, the nephew of one of the survivors who've come to see Peter's film. A wealthy crowd, most of them have drivers waiting for them outside. A few Filipino members of the press, a couple of historians, and a woman hawking her book about the war, round out the crowd.

"This guy's telling a wonderful story," Peter tells me, pointing to Jess Cabarus, a man in his sixties dressed formally in a barong tagalog. Peter says this with a kind of boyish tone and grin. But the story is not wonderful in the way a meal is wonderful or a trip somewhere exciting. Here is the wonderful story: the Japanese came to the place where Jess and his family were living, separated the men from the women and children, then started raping the women. "There were about a hundred and fifty people gathered together," Peter says. "Later, they took a direct hit from an American shell and that took care of about thirty or forty of them,"—"them" meaning not the Japanese, but the refugees.

"Jesus," says Peter. "There are people alive who went through this." It's wonderful in that sense.

But the people gathered around the dining room in small groups seem relaxed, even jocular, as they recount their stories to one another. The horror of it doesn't show in their demeanor. They *could* be talking about movies they've seen, meals they've eaten. My aunt Rose, an aunt by marriage, told me once when I was a boy about Auschwitz after I asked about the blue tattoo on her wrist. While serving me strudel, she told of the Germans shaving her head, prying away her fingernails. What always seemed remarkable to me was not so much the fact of her survival, but how sweet she always seemed, how I could never detect a trace of bitterness.

I'm standing in a group with Jess Cabarus and Peter now, famished, eating anything passed before me by one of the waitstaff. Jess Cabarus, sipping a mango shake, mentions how he was in Vietnam during the Tet Offensive, and how when he saw the firefights erupt in the middle of Saigon, he suddenly was transported back to the fall of Manila. The horror of such experiences always lingers close to the surface, even as one goes about one's life. Peter tells us about going to Japan with his mother in the early seventies to attend the Olympics. As they were walking one day, a boy burst out of a door into the street, then a man chased after him and yelled, "Kura!" (Halt). Peter's mother froze, went nearly "catatonic," and Peter had to lead her away. "I never want to hear that word again," she whispered, stricken, to her son.

The only guest I know besides Peter, his wife, Tea, and Peter's brother and sister-in-law, is the well-known Filipino writer Frankie Sionil José, eighty-two years old, portly, wearing a beret. The twenty-year-old nephew of a survivor is introduced to Frankie José. "He's reading all of your books now at the university," the man tells Jose.

"My apologies," Jose says. A moment later, when someone mentions that this is an exclusive first showing of Peter's film, Jose pipes in, "If I'm invited, it can't be exclusive."

I chat a bit with Jose, his wife, Teresita, and Lourdes Reyes Montinola, one of the board of directors of Far Eastern University, my wife's alma mater. Not that it matters, but it's the only point of common ground I've found tonight, so I sneak the information in. "I always say that FEU is my alma mater, too," says Frankie "because that's where the Kempeitai sequestered me." It's funny, but it's not funny; the Kempeitai were the Japanese version of the Gestapo.

When the film finally begins, I see a different side of Frankie, a different side of all the people in this room. "After what the Japanese did to Manila," Frankie says in the film, "they deserved Hiroshima."

Strong words, but we see what's behind them, a steady parade of gruesome images and eyewitness accounts: women bayoneted in the breasts, babies thrown up in the air and caught as sport on the tips of bayonets, a smiling Japanese soldier holding a head, people burned alive by the dozens, beheaded and shot and stabbed by the thousands. What I had heard before was that the cornered Japanese marines went on a rampage, and that rogue soldiers were responsible for most of the atrocities. This wasn't a systematic plan. Some people believe that American shells caused most of the deaths. But Peter's film pretty neatly does away with such myths, displaying various documents showing that the Japanese, humiliated by their defeat and angered at the lack of cooperation with their rule by the subjugated Filipinos, decided to raze the city and kill everything that moved. Setting fires block by block, the soldiers waited until women and children and men fled into the streets, then shot them or brought them to "beheading factories," not wanting to waste bullets. If one can imagine such a thing, the film shows photos of botched beheadings, men with deep gashes in the backs of their necks who survived, only God knows how, by falling into a pile of corpses. This could be a training film for ISIS, or a rebuke: *You think your murderous techniques are shocking. You're amateurs compared to the Japanese military of World War II.*

Mostly, the people in the room are silent, though every now and then I hear a gasp. Not far from me sits a ninety-five-year-old woman named Jessie Lichauco whose eyes are riveted. She shakes her head infinitesimally.

The film is not vengeful, despite Frankie José's strong remarks. The most the survivors in the film seem to want is an apology from Japan, something it has never officially done, though the Japanese ambassador to the Philippines recently offered his personal apology. So what is the good of remembering? I still wonder, as I watch the film. Wouldn't we rather be at the mayor's birthday bash by the bay? A warped echo of history, his fireworks boom outside the walls of the Adriatico Arms.

When the film ends, we do what all survivors must do—we eat. We feast on a meal I can't even remember now, though I'm sure it was wonderful. We mill about in wonder. Toni Parsons, the wife of Peter's brother Patrick, tells me about feeling the bullet hole in the head of one of the survivors—shot when he was just a boy by the Japanese. I sit next to the ninety-five-year-old Jessie and across from Sara Medina, an American expat who now runs the "Bulletin of the

American Historical Association in Manila." Jessie asks Sara what brought her to the Philippines.

"I married a Filipino," Sara says. "And I came here eleven years ago, and then he died almost as soon as we arrived."

"At least he saved you the expense of bringing his body back," Jessie says.

Jessie is the one who's hard of hearing, but for a moment, it's Sara who looks as though she needs a hearing aid.

"Look, you don't get to be ninety-five without a sense of humor," Jessie tells Sara in a tough-as-nails ninety-five-year-old voice. I take this as good news. I take this as meaning I will live to be a thousand.

Later, she leans over to me. "There's no reason we survived," she says. "We were no smarter than anyone else. I guess we were good at staying out of the way. I knew Peter's mother, father, and grandmother. His grandmother was taken away and we never heard from her again. I had a cousin seven months pregnant. The Japanese took her away and we never heard from her again either. It's not an experience you'd want to live through, but you learn an awful lot about yourself."

It's getting late and I'm maybe the only person in this room without a car and driver. Unlike them, I have to brave the streets of Manila, flag down a cab, and hope the driver doesn't mug me on the long ride home to my apartment in Quezon City. Whenever you get into a cab in Manila you're taking your life in your hands. I've had two cabbies fall asleep at the wheel. I had to wake them up. I've had one cab driver lose his brakes. We coasted into a wall. And I've heard the horror stories of cabbies driving foreigners and Filipinos alike to deserted streets where a confederate awaits to mug and perhaps kill them.

Jessie offers to let me stay at her house, but I thank her and decline. "Are you used to cabs here?" she asks with concern. I assure her I'll be fine and head off into the night.

On the ride home, the streets grow dark and deserted, and I don't recognize the way at all. The driver has seen me in the rearview mirror stupidly taking out my money belt and counting bills. I'm carrying too much, almost two hundred dollars. It doesn't help when I ask him in Tagalog which way we're going and he replies in a low voice, "We're taking a shortcut. It's nearby." I ask him again which way we're going, then I take out my cell phone and dial my brother-in-law's number. No answer. "Shortcut," the cab driver says again. "Nearby." And then he seems not to pay attention to me at all—we're whizzing through streets that hours ago were clogged with the mayor's birthday bash traffic. I dial my sister-in-law's number and she answers. I tell her the nearby landmarks and she assures me I'm headed in the right direction. When I finally arrive at the apartment, I'm so relieved to still be alive that I give the driver an enormous tip as though he's the Angel of Death and he's given me another few hours reprieve before my appointed time.

*

A month later, I'm in another taxi, going to another event of remembrance—no longer in Manila, but in Berlin, another city virtually leveled during World War II. My friend Gregory Maertz has invited me to a show he's helped curate at the Deutsches Historisches Museum on "Art and Propaganda." The opening of the show starts at 6 p.m. and I've arrived at Tegel Airport at 4:45, had just enough time to grab my luggage, check into my hotel, grab a quick shower, and take another taxi to the DHM on Unter den Linden, Berlin's most famous boulevard. Although Berlin is bankrupt, the city is going through an astonishing reconstruction—sixty some years after the war ended, the razed buildings are rising again. The buildings along Unter den Linden, including the Deutsches Historisches Museum, look ancient, but they're only a few years old. This is the East part of Berlin. Doric columned buildings topped by grimy statues line the street. A massive cathedral as big as Canterbury sits on the bank of the river as though it's always stood there. Nearby, the old East German parliament, described as one of the ugliest buildings ever constructed, is being torn down. In its place, a replica of the palace that once stood here before the East Germans dismantled it will be restored, brick by brick: a residence as big as Buckingham Palace. Other buildings in the process of renovation, soon to be corporate headquarters of German companies, are covered with billowing drapes that depict what they will eventually look like. Many of these buildings are fortunate to have suffered the neglect of the East Germans rather than the zeal of the Allies and West Germans, who largely bulldozed what the bombs hadn't destroyed and put up the uninspired architecture of the fifties and sixties. Still, many buildings are pocked with hundreds of bullet holes. It isn't difficult walking among them to imagine the intensity of the struggle that must have been waged here, though now the city is the epitome of cultured calm.

I'm about twenty minutes late when the taxi lets me off in front of the DHM, once the Prussian royal armory. While I don't know exactly where the talk is being held, I spot a clutch of well-dressed men and women talking to a guard who points them around the building. I decide to follow the harried German group, figuring we must be late for the same thing. Around the side of the building is an I. M. Pei addition of glass that I enter along with the group as though I belong to them. I follow them down one escalator, up another, then into a lovely inner courtyard crowded with well-dressed men and women of middle age and an even number of student types, probably about four hundred in all. Not understanding German, I stand attentive in the back of the crowd listening to a speaker at a microphone talk, presumably about the exhibit. I scan the crowd for my friend Greg Maertz but can't see him.

I imagine a similar scene with Hitler addressing a crowd of art patrons, as he often did, here or in Munich, which he designated as the Third Reich's City of Art, art being one of the central pillars of the Nazi regime. But I would never compare these contemporary Germans to their forbearers. Unlike in Manila, this is not a gathering of survivors, but of inheritors of all the legacies of the people who once destroyed this city. I listen to speaker after speaker, not understanding more than a few words, more attuned to the reactions of the students nearby who sometimes shrug and laugh as though they too have no idea what is being said or why. When the official program is over, champagne is served to the entire crowd.

Why have I come here, I wonder—not simply to sip champagne and mingle with people I can't understand. While it's true I'm working on a novel that has something to do with art and propaganda in Germany, this trip wasn't necessary for that. Still, I believe in the idea of *bashert*, the Yiddish word for destiny or fate, that if you are receptive you will learn things you didn't know you needed to know.

The next day, when I meet up with Greg, he tells me the gist of the speeches. A politician spoke first and said that art and politics must never again mix as they did in the Third Reich. He was followed by a French academic who pointed out that art and politics have always mixed and always will. Then he takes me around the exhibit, which doesn't only focus on Nazi propaganda, but places it side by side with Russian, Italian, and American propaganda of the time. The aim isn't to show they're all the same because they're not. A painting of Hitler portrays him as the embodiment of the state, standing proudly in military regalia. A Futurist painting of Mussolini shows Il Duce in myriad profiles of strength and determination, and a painting of Stalin depicts him amid bucolic fields as the national breadwinner. It's morning again in Russia, this painting seems to announce. In contrast, a painting of Roosevelt shows him sitting mildly at a desk with some bit of legislation in front of him, looking more like a minor functionary than a god.

What's remarkable about this exhibit, at least to me, is what people are ready to see and when they're ready to see it. Included are paintings and sculpture from the Nazi era that have not been viewed since those days but have been in cold storage at various depots around Germany and in America because no one knew what to do with them. Some had been confiscated at the end of World War II by the U.S. military; and while many of the paintings have since been returned to Germany, the U.S. Army still holds about 450 of these paintings as war booty in Washington DC, among them the most iconic images of the Nazis. A famous painting of Hitler as a knight on horseback was lent for this exhibit. It has gashes where soldiers used it for bayonet practice. But other less iconic, still controversial, paintings are in the show, such as a painting that Hitler owned, famous in its time, *The Judgment of Paris*, by Ivo Saliger. In the painting, Paris, who looks a little like Edward VIII, is dressed in a Hitler Youth uniform (shorts and pullover shirt, his hair closely cropped), viewing the three naked goddesses from the vantage point of a rock, one arm balanced on his knee. One goddess has her back turned. Another is putting on or taking off her white goddess robe. And a third, who looks a little like Wallis Simpson, stands nude in front of the apprising young man, her palms out, an expression on her face that seems to say, "I can't find anything that matches."

This painting could never be shown as a work of art in Germany, but only in its present context as an historical artifact. Should the same hold true of all the reconstructed buildings of contemporary Berlin, including the Reichstag itself, now once again the seat of German power as it was in Hitler's day? In Munich, Hitler's old luxury apartment is now, fittingly, a police station, and the House of German Art he built there, while still an art museum, houses only art that Hitler himself would have loathed. Shouldn't the Reichstag then be, say, the international headquarters of Amnesty International? But Berlin doesn't seem to get it—history, I mean. The headquarters of the army in Hitler's day is now once again the headquarters of the army. Most of the old Nazi buildings, the ones that survived, are once again government ministries, including Hermann Göring's headquarters of the Luftwaffe, which now, perhaps in a slight ironic gesture, holds the Internal Revenue Service of Germany.

What people see is determined by what they remember. What they remember is determined by what they admit.

Greg shows me a small poster of a blond man, a blonde woman, and a blonde child looking blondely at the horizon. The picture seems so innocuous to me I would have passed over it had Greg not stopped in front.

"We had to cover up this picture while the exhibit was being set up."

I wonder why. Certainly, I understand this bunch was the ideal Aryan family during the Nazi era, but that seems no surprise to me. It's what one would expect to see in a show like this.

"No, the workers putting up the show would find this so offensive," Greg says. "It shows the worst kind of racial profiling. The Germans find it really offensive."

"What about that?" I say, pointing across the way to two ghastly caricatures of Jews in posters of the era, warning of the ill intentions of evil, money-grubbing, long-nosed, baby-eating bloodsuckers. Like me! I'm not saying I would have covered up any of them, but these posters seem at least as offensive to me.

"The Germans are proud they can show that," Greg says. I don't press further, but perhaps I should because it puzzles me. Still, I don't want to make Greg the spokesperson for Germany's complex view of itself. But it intrigues me that the vilification of Jews is, if not innocuous, at least foreign and distant enough as to be viewed neutrally, while the reflection of the National Ideal as portrayed in the 1930s and '40s, is still almost too upsetting to admit.

The next day I book a tour of Berlin with a company called Enigma Tours. Although Enigma Tours is more expensive than the rest, they seem a little less impersonal in that the tours are not conducted on large tour buses, but small minivans with a longtime resident native English speaker. As I'm always up for an enigma, and I'm forever trying to prove the adage that a fool and his money are soon parted, I throw in my lot with Enigma.

My tour guide is a white South African named Guy with a bad cold and a bilious attitude toward everyone from the Turkish immigrants in Germany ("There's no love lost between them and the Germans," he tells us. "They're Muslims besides. Not exactly the flavor of the month, you know"), to politicians (on passing the Reichstag, he points out stones that represent the politicians Hitler had killed: "You can't kill enough politicians in my opinion," Guy tells us. "He should have killed more," which might seem funny if there was anything funny about it).

By chance, or perhaps bashert, it happens to be the anniversary of the liberation of Auschwitz, what's now known as Holocaust Remembrance Day. I didn't realize this until this morning when I turned on CNN. I think, of course, about my aunt Rose, and the biggest enigma of all: how to this day she remains the most cheerful person I've ever met. Her entire family was killed, except for her son, who was separated from her when they arrived at the camp. Both assumed the other was dead until ten years after the war when they ran into each other by chance, or perhaps bashert, on a street in Tel Aviv. I thought not only of Rose but of the survivors I met in Manila, Frankie José and ninety-five-year-old Jessie Lichauco, both of them with their senses of humor intact despite what they endured. Still, it's hard for me to imagine living through something like that and being able to go beyond that moment—like Peter Parson's mother being recalled to the moment of trauma by the word, "Kura!" For me, I imagine, it would always be that moment. I would never escape it.

Guy zips us around Berlin—there are seven of us in the van. I'm sitting in the front with Guy, and I hardly look around to see my fellow Enigmas except to hand back the postcards of bombed out Berlin that Guy passes around to give us context. We pass by the remains of Hitler's bunker, the place where he shot himself, which is now a parking lot and which, remarkably, had no marking at all until six months ago when a sign was put up. I suppose they didn't want the place to become a shrine for neo-Nazis, but there's no sense in denying that such people exist who would make it such a shrine. These people exist, and maybe even thrive, whether we want them to or not. We are powerless against their collective forgetting.

When we arrive at the relatively new Holocaust Memorial, Guy tells us there are 2,700 stones that make up the memorial, though he doesn't know why. "I don't think the number has any significance," he tells us. I don't know why, either, but I can see the power of this field of uneven stones, a field of gravestones, lopped off unevenly, or buildings razed, an eternal battlefield.

"This memorial is pretty controversial," he tells us. "A lot of people don't feel it's inclusive enough. They feel it's too narrow. Half of the Nazis victims weren't Jewish, but gypsies, homosexuals, the mentally retarded." My sense is that Guy's concern isn't so much driven by compassion for any of these groups as it is a kind of free-floating resentment toward Jews. Guy doesn't strike me as the type who would put up a memorial to anyone.

From the back of the van, a man pipes up. "We Poles feel quite strongly about this issue," he says.

"I bet you do," says Guy, who fumbles for a tissue and coughs into it. Guy is looking pretty rough for a tour guide—his shoulders sag, his eyes are bleary, and his thin hair is pasted to his brow. He curses at a woman who changes lanes abruptly in front of him, then goes into another coughing jag.

No one knows I'm Jewish and I wonder if I should say anything. I wonder if I should mention that a Holocaust memorial to the Jews, unarguably the prime target of Hitler's Final Solution, does not preclude memorials to other victims of the Nazis. When I visited Dachau a couple of years ago, I was moved by all the memorials, including a small plaque to six British nurses, I believe, who were killed at Dachau late in the war. It seems to me that the problem with suffering, the problem with remembering suffering, is that there is no end to the one while the other is all too finite. I want to acknowledge to the Polish man, so affronted by the Holocaust Memorial here, that indeed the Poles suffered greatly at the hands of the Nazis and later at the hands of the Soviets. Nor were the Poles blameless when it came to making Jews suffer, and it took little encouragement by the Nazis to fan the flames of Polish antisemitism, as Princeton professor Jan Gross's books on Polish pogroms attest.

I'm debating whether to say anything, or whether I should let the moment pass, when Guy speaks up again. "But you know the artist who did this was an American and the Americans are very narrow on this subject."

"Yes, they are!" says an American voice. "Very narrow!" I glance back and see the man who spoke is a middle-aged black man.

I'm dumbfounded and I decide that I will keep my identity, and my view of suffering, to myself. I'm afraid that this is going to turn into a discussion about how Jews control the media, the government, inevitably the banks. I'm afraid I might get my wish and tumble into a different time period, too terrible to survive. How easy it is to sit comfortably doing nothing and still be exterminated. All you need is to find yourself riding in the wrong vehicle in a strange city, or a city once familiar, but no longer. All you need is to be noticed by the wrong person.

Finally, I say to Guy, "You know, I think this is actually Holocaust Remembrance Day."

He gives me a blank look. "Yeah, maybe. Okay. Maybe that's why so many flags are at half-staff."

As we leave the Holocaust Memorial for another irrelevant site in this newly refurbished city, I do what I always do: I wonder. I wonder what my fate would have been in this city during wartime. Actually, I don't wonder. I know. If lucky enough (well, beyond luck, luck multiplied so many times as to become bashert) I would have wound up staring wide-eyed at my liberators as I crowded against the fence. I would have thought, What is the use of remembering when all history is mute? From this question, I would have cultivated impossibly optimistic attitudes. I would have imagined myself laughing again, feasting, sipping champagne among my former tormentors.

6. Naomi Hemley celebrating Canada Day. Courtesy of the author.

Independence Days

Several hundred people dressed in red and white have turned out today at Diefenbaker Park, a large expanse of hills and dales with a pond, a forest, gardens, and a waterfall. Activity tents dot the flat span of grass by the road, where cars are lined for a kilometer or more. Under one tent, two huge red and white cakes adorned with maple leaves await patriotic consumption, but that will be a while yet, so my two young daughters and I wait in line for free hot dogs while "The Good Old Hockey Song," which sounds old to my ears, if not good, and which everyone but my team of interlopers knows by heart, blasts from the hot dog truck and everyone around us joins in. I display my support for Canada, on this, its national day, by drinking a Canada Dry Ginger Ale while my eleven-year-old daughter, Shoshie, has her face painted with a maple leaf and someone writes CANADA across the forehead of my seven-year-old daughter, Naomi, in jagged crayon, which makes her look like the victim of a psycho killer. (Jason with his good old hockey mask comes to mind.)

I've rented a house for the July Fourth weekend just across the border in Point Roberts, and as Canada Day comes three day before my own national day celebration, we've decided to infiltrate Canada for its celebration. Our vacation rental would be only a ten-minute drive from Diefenbaker Park if there wasn't an international border between them, but there is, and that's the point of Point Roberts, an exclave of the United States, dangling off the tip of Canada below the forty-ninth parallel. Logically, Point Roberts should belong to

Canada, but it doesn't. During the seven years in the nineties I lived in Bellingham, Washington, across two international borders from Point Roberts, I sometimes heard rumors of the place, like some lost colony, but I never visited.

When it comes time for the giant maple leaf cakes to be cut, most people in the park converge upon the shelter that houses the cakes. A man in a yellow vest from the Lions Club, which sponsors the event, has the thankless job of thanking the local grocery store for the cakes, the DQ for the five hundred hot dogs, the Tsawwassen Pathfinders, and "the people who take care of the balloons." A man and a woman decked out in the regalia of the Royal Canadian Mounted Police stand by and absorb much of my attention as I flip easily to a boyhood fascination with Mounties. (What could be more Canadian than Mounties in full dress?) Then the politicians speak of the things that politicians like to speak of: patriotism, sacrifice, and the bindings that bind us together into that mysterious binder of national identity that supposedly holds us in place. A member of parliament, Carol Ann Findley, recalls that the RCMP has had a tough year, a number of deaths in the field, and she thanks the members of the armed forces, finishing by proclaiming as one does on one's national day that "Canada is the best country in the world. Yay, Canada," and the crowd cheers. When it's the mayor of Tsawwassen's turn to speak, she asks the people in attendance to "celebrate who we are, our shared values." *I share your values*, I want to chime in. *Can I be an honorary Canadian? My kids go to the Canadian School in Singapore.* Her speech, the Mounties, the cake, even my introduction to "The Good Old Hockey Song" combine to make me feel proud to masquerade as a Canadian until a children's choir leads us all in "O, Canada," first in French, then in English, and a woman in front of me grouses, "They should have sung it in English first." I know none of the words to either the French or the Canadian versions except for "O, Canada," which I belt out all the same like some deranged Yank, which is of course what I am.

Between versions, Shoshie chimes in loudly, "I don't know this song."

"Don't advertise that," I say. With her face painted with Canadian maple leaf and flag, holding a red balloon, and a Canada pin pinned to her book bag, I must seem like a terrible Canadian parent, not even teaching my child the national anthem.

But maybe I'm a terrible American parent because Shoshie admits not knowing the American national anthem, the one with all the question marks, though she does know "America, the Beautiful" which she sings at full volume as we march up the hill toward our car parked a kilometer away.

I tell her I'm not loyal, at least not to countries, partly to get her to stop singing.

"Which country would you fight for?" she asks. "The U.S. or Canada?"

"It depends," I say. "I'm usually for the underdog."

"What if Canada decided to take back Point Roberts by force?"

"Then I'd probably be for America because I don't believe in aggression. But if it were the other way around, I'd be for Canada."

"I wouldn't want to be in an alliance with you, Dad," she finally concludes.

"Unfortunately you are. You're my daughter."

Signs warn us not to block the driveways of the Canadians whose houses line the road as we wait in line on our way back to Point Roberts. These people seem to have all the hassles but none of the benefits of living next to Point Roberts, their constant view is a steady stream of cars and occasional fistfights. A woman in a Lexus in front of us learns too late that the lane for frequent border crossers is closed, so she tries to nudge in front of a pickup truck with Washington plates. Hers are Canadian plates, and perhaps both of them own property in Point Roberts: he, I'm guessing, a voter, she, merely a taxpayer. That makes all the difference in the world in Point Roberts. The Point Roberts Taxpayers Association once explored the idea of merging with the Point Roberts Voters Association some years back, but ultimately the voters wanted to husband this last vestige of, well, not "difference" because Canadians by and large bristle when Americans say Canadians are no different from Americans. (But really, hockey? That's where you want to stake your claim? Okay, *viva la difference!*) Let's just say the true blue Americans in Point Roberts wanted to keep their sense of privilege separate. Anyone can be a taxpayer, but only Americans can vote in American elections.

Technically, Point Roberts is not a pure exclave, as it's possible to sail a boat from one of the San Juan Islands to Point Roberts and never leave U.S. coastal waters, but I don't own a boat. Most people who travel to Point Roberts, or away from it, travel by land. And because it's cut off from the rest of the U.S. without actually being an island, it's hard to be here without thinking constantly of borders.

If it were part of Canada, it would look just like Tsawwassen, which isn't ugly, but simply ordinary with its string of Tim Hortons, London Drugs, Dairy Queens, candy stores, gas stations, shopping malls, and busy intersections that line a drag for miles, a nearly endless carpet of commerce, until the border where it just ends. This is what the border has done to Point Roberts. It has, in a sense, saved it, if salvation lies in its ruralness, its wooded lots and forest trails, its beaches and the four parks that anchor each corner, the eagles that nest there, the unhurried lifestyle. If salvation lies in that.

The man in the pickup rams the car trying to nudge in and the girls and I gasp. The woman in the Lexus sits in place in shock. I, with no guarded borders of my own in this place, allow her to cut.

On the mile and a half walk from our million-dollar beachfront rental to the Point Roberts Community Center, a heron flies over and a baby rabbit scurries through the brush on the side of the mostly empty street we walk along. Shoshanna has been in the mode of "Hurry up or all the pancakes will be gone" since waking, even though it's not even nine yet, but her younger sister Naomi can't be hurried. Naomi might have spent the morning happily "painting" a rock she found with a carnation, but I made her save it for later. Next, she bends to pick up roly-polies for her "collection."

When we finally reach the low-slung red brick community center, the tableau seems deceptively American: a slate board advertising the Fourth of July breakfast to the occasional passing car, an American flag fluttering on its pole. In the community center basement, decorated with faux wood tables, chairs, and a hybrid mix of about forty-five Canadians and Americans, I recognize Kandace Harper who retired here with her husband from California because Point Roberts reminded them of Cabot's Cove, the fictional Maine setting of *Murder She Wrote*. I met them last January on my first extended visit to the Point and, after I left, she provided me with a slew of documents about the controversial radio towers that are set to be built here. She's part of the "Cross Border Coalition" of residents from Point Roberts and Tsawwassen fighting the towers, which will cause "blanket interference" to wireless and other communications for the residents of Point Roberts and Tsawwassen, a bedroom community of Vancouver of twenty-three thousand residents. To me, it seems like an eleventh-hour fight. What can this small community do against the powerful businessmen who own the radio stations?

When Punjabi radio station, Sher-E-Punjab, broadcasting from Richmond, British Columbia, decided to move its radio towers from Ferndale, Washington to just within the international border on the

Point Roberts side, the idea was to boost its radio signal to 50,000 kW to serve its hundreds of thousands of Indian listeners in the Greater Vancouver area. Because of their proximity to the border and lax Canadian regulations, the owners have been able to operate in a communications No Man's Land. Without a license from the Canadian Radio-television and Telecommunications Commission (their applications for licenses for their stations have repeatedly been denied by the CRTC), they created a holding company in the U.S., BBC Broadcasting Inc., with an American as the primary stockholder, as well as a shell American radio station, KRPI, which leases its radio towers back to Sher E Punjab. In its application to the FCC in Washington, BBC Broadcasting submitted a map that entirely omitted Tsawwassen.

After indulging our God-given American right to all-you-can-eat breakfasts, we head to the playground out back to deal with our sugar highs as appropriate to our age and station: my girls by running madly about the park with two other kids their age, me sitting very still in a sugar coma by the playground. Striking up a conversation with the parents of Shoshie and Naomi's new friends, Eric and Jeanine, a couple in their late thirties or early forties, I learn that Eric's family owns a cottage in Point Roberts—they've had it for thirty-five years and they visit Point Roberts, like so many Canadians—because the place is so different from where they live. Seventy-five percent of the homeowners here are Canadians, which means that over 60 percent of the cottages here are unoccupied during the off-season. In the language of the border, these are always cottages. Even mansions are "cottages," a term that suggests vacation, impermanence. If you're Canadian, you're always visiting your cottage in Point Roberts, never going home.

"This place is untouched," Jeanine tells me. Her mother-in-law says it's the same way it was thirty-five years ago. And the culture is so different from Canada, so different from Chilliwack, where they won't even let their kids walk downtown or play in the yard alone. Here, the kids are out with flashlights playing capture the flag after dark. When she enters Pt. Roberts, she really feels like she's in another country.

"American junk food is so different from ours," she says, which elicits from me a laugh, but not from Eric.

"It's so different," he says, inscrutable behind his reflective Harley glasses.

Shoshie, Naomi, and the Canadian couple's kids, Brenna and Gracie, all pause in their play to glorify American junk food, reciting the list like articles of faith: "Cherry Dr Pepper, Almond Joy, Mounds, Reese's Peanut Butter spread, Eggo Waffles, Kool-Aid."

"I've never had Kool-Aid," Shoshie says.

"Tell your dad it's twenty-five cents a packet," Eric says.

"But it takes half a cup of sugar," Jeanine says.

Perhaps I've idealized Canada in the way that they idealize America. It's not just American junk food they worship, thank God, but the down-homeness that pancake breakfasts and Fourth of July parades represent. In my experience, places that are down home are often exclusionary and xenophobic. *It's my down home, not yours.* In this gated community, perhaps *the* most gated community in North America, its one thousand three hundred residents enjoy the protection of American and Canadian border guards. But it's undeniably down home, if down homeness includes a feeling of safety, of being able to allow your kids to run around, and being able to leave your car unlocked with the engine running. Where is a car thief going to go when he's only got eight square miles to roam and everyone knows his neighbor and his neighbor's car?

But the word from Chilliwack is not good. That bucolic Northwest lifestyle I imagine in British Columbia has migrated away from Chilliwack at least. During salmon fishing season, fishermen enact a witless parody of the Great Outdoors, standing shoulder-to-shoulder along the river casting upstream, tangling their lines, and getting into fistfights. Such a treat to be out in nature, eh? It's sport for Eric and Jeanine to watch this "craziness" from a safe distance.

I comment to Eric that everyone in Point Roberts seems to be from Canada. "Look at the license plates," Eric says, pointing to the cars lining the community center parking lot. "Oh, there's one from Washington."

We leave Eric posed like Lady Liberty, trying to find the best spot for cell coverage. In the liminal space of Point Roberts, cell coverage from my American provider and Eric's Canadian provider are equally iffy. "I've got two bars," he cries out joyously as we leave him.

Untouched, Jeanine said. *This place is untouched*. Not really. There's a colonial-era map in Liberty Hall in Philadelphia in which the cartographer only concerned himself with the Eastern Seaboard of what would become the United States. Beyond that, the Allegheny chain was simply labeled "Endless Mountains." In similar fashion, the map BBC Broadcasting filed showed none of the streets of Tsawwassen lined with London Drugs, Tim Hortons, health clubs, gas stations, Dairy Queens, liquor stores, and hundreds of houses inhabited by twenty-three thousand residents. In their place was a blank spot, an erasure, terra nullius.

The FCC has already approved the application, and the radio stations have been operating for years without a license because the politicians in Vancouver want to woo the Indian vote. Who would dare cross an organization, illegal or not, that represents hundreds of thousands of votes? And it's not as though the three Punjabi stations are the only pirate stations in Canada. There are others in Montreal with radio towers in Vermont. The director of Radio India, Maninder Gill, who allegedly shot a Sikh man in the leg in a parking lot (self-defense, his lawyers claim), and whose house was later riddled with machine gun fire, threatens to "fill the roads" with fifty thousand people if anyone tries to shut him down.

For many years of its history, the border was barely acknowledged by residents on either side; before the midsixties, the border was maintained on the honor system, when two roads into Point Roberts existed, the Upper and Lower borders, and a sign at the Lower border stated that if you had anything to declare, you should turn around and use the Upper Border. Not that anyone took that sign seriously back then, but even so, what they might have smuggled didn't matter much by today's standards. In the days of the porous border, most people used Canadian currency. If you had to pay duty to American customs, good luck finding someone to exchange your Canadian dollars for greenbacks. The post office had them, but they wouldn't sell you any. If you worked for Neilson Lumber in Point Roberts, say, and you owed duty on some building materials you were bringing across, the border guard might just reach in his pocket, pull out a wad of singles, and say, "Tell old man Neilson that he owes me six bucks." Go back further than that, and you'd have Point Roberts schoolchildren singing "God Save the Queen" before "The Star-Spangled Banner" and children let out of school for the queen's birthday. What porousness still survives is in the hybridized attitudes of people on the both sides of the border, in the many "mixed marriages" of Canadians and Americans, and in the gardens of the Canadians whose houses line the other side of the border. Bike along Roosevelt Way and you'll see the gates in the fence to allow Canadians to visit their gardens in the U.S. They walk out the back gate, cross an imaginary line, pick their peas and beans, then return to Canada. Before 9/11, many of the Canadians had planks across the ditch along the border and used to wheel their garden waste and throw it where the golf course is now. Or they'd walk their dogs in America. But no more. No one crosses that ditch now.

"I have a dual identity," Fred Culbert, whose father first bought a cottage in Point Roberts in 1943, told me on my first visit in January. "Not dual citizenship. When I cross the border—I live in Tsawwassen. It's ten minutes from my house in Canada to the border—I flip a switch and become an American. When I walk into the Shell station in the morning for a cup of coffee, I talk like the boys, walk like them, and spit like them. I stop saying 'aboot' and try to say 'about.'"

This is exactly how I want to feel when I visit Point Roberts, or Tsawwassen, or anywhere else I feel a connection, a polygamist of place. Not divided loyalties, but multiple loyalties.

From the community center, Shoshie, Naomi, and I walk another half kilometer to Brewster's, the kind of boutiquey-yet-homey restaurant you might find in any hip town from Halifax to Monterrey. Galen Wood, the sister of writer Gretel Ehrlich, hosted me on my visit in January, and has invited us to watch the parade from the table in front of Brewster's she's reserved for her family and friends. She's American and first came to Point Roberts with her husband, a Canadian in the 1960s, but her son and his kids are Canadian and live in Langley. In this sense, her story is like almost everyone else's in Point Roberts. When people are introduced at parties, the first question is inevitably some variation of "How did you end up here?"

As we make introductions all around, one of Galen's friends, Annelle Norman, who moved from Denver to Point Roberts because she "fell in love with the place" says to my daughters, "Welcome to Point Roberts. It doesn't get any more American than this." Galen and Annelle are the only two Americans besides myself and my daughters at this hybridized table of twelve, so the remark seems a bit odd in the literal sense.

Peter Courtney, a Canadian who lives on Bowen Island near Vancouver beside her, gently objects, "Well, there's a flavor of maple syrup running through it."

Just as Annelle asks me what I think of Point Roberts, five kids, eight to twelve years old, hollering and waving small American flags, run down the empty street, an informal advance guard of the parade. A few people in lawn chairs give them a wave and a desultory cheer.

One of the kids yells in our general direction, "Happy Fourth. Woo hoo. Even though we're Canadian."

I'm seated next to Carol Clark, who lives in Tsawwassen. Both she and Annelle are curious about my impressions.

"I see this as a hybrid place," I say. Not a difficult assessment to make. Even some in the crowd along the parade route carry hybridized flags that are half Stars and Stripes, half Maple Leaf.

But Carol likes this word, "hybrid," and tells me that Point Roberts never had permanent residents. The natives of the area would use it as fishing grounds. At Lily Point, where one of Point Roberts's four parks is located, there was a comingling of the types of fishing that were done here by the various tribes. The Halkomelem speakers from the Fraser River Delta used bag nets to catch salmon, while the Straits speakers from the San Juan–Gulf Islands used reef nets. As early as 1791, European explorers noted the productive fisheries of these tribes and their seasonal occupation of Point Roberts, or Chelhtenem, as it was once called by the Central Coast Salish Indians. As late as 1881, the *Washington Standard* reported that ten thousand salmon were caught in three native reef nets in one six hour period.

"Do you know what it means to be tarred and feathered?" Peter, a former British Columbia school administrator, asks Shoshie.

She doesn't, so he explains that one of his ancestors during the American Revolution was a "United Empire Loyalist," and was subjected to the favorite form of revolutionary humiliation: being covered in pine tar and feathers by the American revolutionaries. He fled to Canada where he and other Loyalist exiles founded the town of St. Andrews by the Sea. Another ancestor helped draw the border between Canada and the U.S.

"You couldn't be sitting next to anyone more Canadian," he tells me.

Peter lives on Bowen Island now, about a twenty-minute ferry ride form Vancouver. An avid trout fisherman, he tells us that the secret places where the big fish live are called "pocket waters."

"This cultural community is so powerful compared to any other place I've ever been. People congregate here intuitively. Point Roberts," he says, "is a pocket water."

Perhaps. It's definitely a pocket of some sort, tucked away, both guarded and unguarded in its sense of identity, but to me, it's birds rather than fish that capture the essence of the place. The salmon are long gone, but the eagles that fed on them remain, at least some. There used to be a heron rookery here, but when the golf course was built the herons flew away and they haven't been back since.

The biggest controversy now are the towers, but there seems to be a difference between my first visit in January and this. I've noticed some resignation about the towers, I say, which makes the two women bristle. Annelle warns against complacency and Carol says, "As I come across the border as a Canadian, I make a practice of seeing the blue skies and the trees that I enjoy so much. We're applying to have Tyee Drive declared a scenic drive. We're applying the principle of what we want to see and working with the local government to see that that takes place. We want this to be a cooperative effort. As far as the FCC is concerned, they've already approved the license, but the county still has to approve the use of the land."

Carol disputes that the golf course, which is near the proposed towers, drove the herons away. She contends that herons naturally move their rookeries from time to time, but if we destroy the land they used in the past, "there won't be any chance of them coming back."

There *can* be cooperative efforts, she insists. One citizen asked the marina to change the location of the fireworks last year to protect some eagle fledglings. And they did so this year.

An eagle flies above us on cue, an adolescent, and she points it out. "If you look at old photographs or lithographs of the tribes fishing, the sky is full of eagles feeding off the scraps," she says. "What a wonderful way to live."

It's not Shangri-la, but this is the only community I know besides the Baarles of Belgium and the Netherlands in which a border has created a sense of hybridity rather than diminished it. There is something admirably odd and sheltered about a place that inspires commitment from people who don't necessarily live within its borders. I'm surrounded by Canadians who are committed to America, or at least one sliver of it. There's Carol, a force in local conservation efforts, and Peter, both of whose loyalties are spacious. Peter gleaned 350 pounds of apples from neglected trees, and donated it to the food bank, but reserved 50 pounds for hard apple cider. When the fruit flies invaded the cider and turned it into vinegar, he sold the vinegar at Christmas to free slaves in Sudan. It's too easy for me to give in to despair and cynicism—but my daughters and I have sufficient food and shelter and freedom of movement, so we should also have the luxury of being able to emerge from our hiding places to act outside our small boundaries and the celebrations of those boundaries.

For me, the example of cross border cooperation between Point Roberts and Tsawwassen, their sense of unity despite their international separation, illustrates something far more powerful than simply a *not-in-my-backyard* dispute. Perhaps there's something in Carol's notion of applying the principle of imagining the world we *want* to see as we cross these reinforced but imagined and ever mutable lines. Some months later, I receive a jubilant email from Galen informing me that the Cross Border Coalition has won its battle and BBC Broadcasting has abandoned its towers project.

As the sky bursts open in our national colors, my childlike delight in fireworks supersedes the symbolism each burst overhead conveys— only in a place of peace can fireworks seem decorative. Only in a place of peace can borders seem merely an inconvenience, the price one pays to live a gated life of nature hikes and mountain vistas.

As Shoshie, Naomi, and I look skyward in anticipation of each burst, I spend as much time gazing away from the fireworks as toward them, across the choppy waters of Boundary Bay at the whale-shaped mountains across the way, a solitary red light on one signaling the only visible human claim on the land. I believe I'm actually staring due south toward Canada, an anomaly in the border due to its dip below the forty-ninth parallel to incorporate all of Vancouver Island, the last concession the American negotiators allowed the English, letting Vancouver Island go but nothing else below the forty-ninth. Shifting my gaze slightly, it's Washington across the water. In the daytime, I'd see snow-capped Mt. Baker dominating the horizon and the town of Blaine, Washington.

A bird hovers in front of my face, at a distance so intimate it could peck my eyes. Does it think I'm a flower? Am I near its nest? I'm not spiritual enough to rate a spirit guide and I'm no Annie Dillard. This bird is not a metaphor for anything. The bird is real, perhaps disoriented by the loud booms and the frazzled lights in the sky, and fleeing low, never expected to be met with an obstacle. For a moment, it seems confined by me, but then it seems to remember its one great advantage and flickers off fast as the fireworks in the direction of international waters.

To order or obtain more information on these or other University of Nebraska Press titles, visit nebraskapress.unl.edu.